# TEACHING
# GODLY PLAY

## The Sunday Morning Handbook

### Jerome W. Berryman

Abingdon Press
Nashvile

TEACHING GODLY PLAY

The Sunday Morning Handbook

*Copyright © 1995 by Abingdon Press*

*This book is printed on recycled, acid-free paper.*

**Library of Congress Cataloging-in-Publication Data**

Berryman, Jerome.
    Teaching godly play : the sunday morning handbook / Jerome W. Berryman.
        p.      cm.
    Includes bibliographical references.
    ISBN 0-687-08651-5 (alk. paper)
    1. Christian education of children. 2. Montessori method of education. I. Title.
    BV1475.2.B47      1995
    268'.432—dc20

                                                                95-16813
                                                                CIP

Scripture quotations, unless otherwise noted, are from the New Revised Standard Version Bible. Copyright © 1989 by the Division of Christian Education of the National Council of Churches of Christ in the USA. Used by permission.

Scripture quotations noted RSV are from the Revised Standard Version of the Bible, copyright 1946, 1952, 1971 by the Division of Christian Education of the National Council of Churches of Christ in the USA. Used by permission.

95  96  97  98  99  00  01  02  03  04 — 10  9  8  7  6  5  4  3  2  1

MANUFACTURED IN THE UNITED STATES OF AMERICA

# Acknowledgments

This book is especially dedicated with deep gratitude to the children, families, teachers, and all the volunteers who helped with our excellent education program at Christ Church Cathedral, 1984–1994. I came there first from the Institute of Religion in the Texas Medical Center as a consultant to set up this program as well as others for all ages, and I stayed for a decade as Canon Educator. The place and the people became my spiritual home and in many ways they still are.

It is not possible to think about this work without remembering my teacher, Sofia Cavalletti. Her generous spirit and profound understanding of religious education still sustains, teaches, and challenges me.

Thea (Mrs. Berryman) is present on every page of this book and informs the work at every level. I am a better teacher when the children are present, so I hope I have not made too many mistakes during my solitary writing about what they have taught us. The mistakes are mine, not hers.

Our whole family has grown up with this. Coleen and Alyda were little girls when we began. They are now young women. Coleen is an artist, and Alyda is a mother and teacher. Alyda and Michael Macaluso are the parents of Alexandra. Now, Thea and I are starting over again, delighting in, playing with, and learning from our granddaughter. They all have helped with this book.

Finally, I would like to thank Jill Reddig of Abingdon Press, who first believed in this book. I also would like to thank Cynthia Gadsden, my editor, and David Ellis, the copy editor. They were a delight to work with, and the book shows it.

*Jerome W. Berryman*
Christmas, 1994

# Contents

# Definitions

The **community of children**—is a way of looking at the children in the classroom. They are more than a group of people in the same place at the same time working under the same rules. They are working together toward the same goal. They are a "body" of different people working together like the different parts of the human body to make a whole, living and growing entity.

Like the human body if you touch this community in a single place the whole organism changes. It is a system. This is why teaching is not thought of as a linear, one billiard ball hitting another, kind of causality. Neither is teaching thought of as using several causes, such as different media for lessons, to produce the same goal. This view of education takes into consideration the whole group as well as the individuals.

The view of the church as "the body of Christ" is the source for this way of looking at the children, and they are seen as ministers as well.

It is expected that the community of children will learn how to maintain itself in a constructive way. This provides early learning about how Christian people live together and what the ministry of the laity feels like.

**The doorperson**—This person does much more than help manage the coming in and the going out of the children. He or she needs special talent to be able to help the children help themselves get out their work. This person also helps the children set up the feast.

**The environment**—was seen by Montessori as critical to meeting children's educational needs. Children from about three to six years need furnishings appropriate to their physical size, so they won't have to waste energy learning to adjust to an adult setting. The furnishings, the teachers, and the rules need to be consistent for the same reason.

The environment also needs to be well cared for. Children learn from this that they and what goes on in that place are valued by the adult leaders.

Other living creatures such as plants and animals give life to the setting for learning. They also provide the occasion for children to care for life. Children also need to be involved in cleaning, restoring to order, and enjoying the setting where their teaching and learning take place.

Montessori wanted children to help prepare the meals and snacks at school. Real gardens to care for and to provide some of the food for the school were considered important for the children's integrated, whole self to develop. Much of this has not been associated with religious education. Perhaps it is not possible on Sunday morning, but it is possible in schools, homes, and sometimes hospitals. Children need to learn constructive ways to communicate with all of life.

As children move beyond the period of early childhood the environment opens up to include other rooms and to incorporate field trips in the neighborhood. Montessori wanted the children to begin to experience a wider and wider area of the real world as they developed the conceptual ability to organize their thinking about these experiences. This is true for the learning and teaching of Christianity as well. It helps children know who they are and the possibilities for ministry in their community.

**The feast**—is a time after the work is put away when the children gather again in the circle. Napkins, cookies, and juice (or other more elaborate things) are put before each child by children, prayers are said, and the the feast is shared. Children think of this as a "snack" but that gives the storyteller the opportunity to say that what makes a feast is how you feel about it. It does not matter what you have to eat.

**Freedom**—is an often misunderstood concept in Montessori. Some think that there is no control of children's actions and others think there is too much control. This comes from only reading parts of Montessori's writings or not noticing how children are guided to make constructive choices.

The more constructive self-direction children have the fewer outside limits they need. When children have little or no self-direction they need carefully planned alternatives presented to them. Sometimes only one choice is given. "You may now get out this work."

Freedom is not the ability to act on impulse. It is the ability to know who you are, where you are going, and to make good choices to get there. Whim can be a tyrant, creating a decision-cripple. Freedom from impulse sets us free to do what God calls us to do. "For you were called to freedom, brothers and sisters; only do not use your freedom as an opportunity for self-indulgence, but through love become slaves to one another" (Galatians 5:13).

**Getting out your work**—is after the lesson. Children are invited to get out their own work to make a response to the day's lesson, or to another issue they are working on. Sometimes there is work already in progress from previous sessions.

**Getting ready**—is any time children are guided toward the ability to focus. This is an important part of what is necessary for the language of religion to perform its function. Christianity invites people into parables, sacred stories, the liturgy, and into silence to become aware of God in an indirect way. If one cannot "enter" this language the awareness of God can remain hidden.

The children especially need to be ready before a lesson begins. The posture for being ready is sitting calmly with ones legs crossed ("Indian style") at the ankles with your hands on your ankles. This is not to be maintained rigidly, but it is a position to come back to in order to reinforce being ready so the lesson can continue.

**Godly Play**—is what Jerome Berryman calls his interpretation of Montessori religious education. His 1991 book *Godly Play: A Way of Religious Education* is an introduction to his views. He graduated in 1972 from the Center for Advanced Montessori Studies in Bergamo, Italy and has wide experience in this form of education as well as religious education. He was trained as a lawyer at Tulsa University Law School and is a member of the American Bar Association Family Law Section. His theological training was at Princeton Theological Seminary. During the last several decades his experience has covered working with sick children, especially at Texas Children's Hospital; working with families, especially at Houston Child Guidance; working in the parish, especially as Canon Educator at Christ Church Cathedral in downtown Houston; and in schools, especially at Holy Spirit Episcopal School in Houston.

**Group wondering**—comes after a lesson in the circle of children. The storyteller may say something like, "I wonder what this could really be," as he or she touches a part of a parable.

Wondering is guided in slightly different ways for parables, sacred stories, liturgical action and silence, and this is discussed in detail in this book.

**Indirect teaching (and learning)**—is indirect in two ways. First, this is teaching that teaches the art of how to discover something. It is a focus on the tools to create a meaningful result rather than directly teaching the children the result without asking them to go through the process of discovering it for themselves. Second, the means to discover something can include the environment for learning and the community of children who are themselves doing the learning. One can teach "through" the way the classroom setting is laid out and through the way the children in that setting are being treated as a group.

**The lesson**—is a presentation to the children, sitting in a circle, by the story-teller. A physical material, representing the parable, sacred story, liturgical action, or silence is used. This is important for the storytelling but also because children of all ages need something concrete for them to focus on while they are reflecting on it. It is difficult to wonder about the lesson when one has to hold it present in the mind. The younger children do not yet have the cognitive ability to do that.

**Materials**—are the physical representations used in the lesson to show the sacred story, the parable, liturgical action, or silence to the children as the lesson is presented and reflected on during the wondering.

**Ministry**—is an action. It involves several conceptual dimensions which need to be taken into consideration to keep it balanced and to provide a continuing corrective critique. This view was developed at Princeton Theological Seminary by the Doctor of Ministry Program.

The four dimensions of ministry include the educational and communications aspect. Second, there is the administrative and organizational aspect. Third is the pastoral care of sustaining persons and the pastoral counseling that helps people change. Finally, there is the theological and ethical dimension. A specific act of ministry, such as the educational act, will "pull" this system of relationships toward its focus of attention, but the other issues of concern cannot be detached. For example, education is deeply involved in communication, but it is also related to acts of pastoral care and counseling, theology and ethics, and the way we lead and organize the act of teaching and learning.

**Montessori**—is a kind of open classroom, developmentally appropriate education begun by Maria Montessori (1870–1952) in 1907 when she opened her first school. She was the first woman to graduate with a medical degree in modern Italy (1896), and in 1910 committed herself entirely to education. Today many of her innovations such as little tables and chairs and the use of manipulatives are completely accepted and Montessori education is widely used in both private and public schools.

**Montessori Religious Education**—is not well known by either Montessorians or by religious educators. Maria Montessori felt that the spiritual formation of the child was at the heart of her work. E. M. Standing (1887–1967) is an example of the second generation of this tradition of religious education. He wrote *Maria Montessori: Her Life and Work* which is still in print and used in Montessori training courses. His *Child in the Church* which reached its final form in 1965, just two years before he died, was a major contribution to religious education.

Sofia Cavalletti is the outstanding representative of the third generation. She is a Hebrew scholar, as well known in Italy for her publications in this field as for her work with Montessori religious education. In 1963 she set up The Maria Montessori Association for the Religious Formation of the Child. Today it is the center of a worldwide organization. In the United States her work is well known as The Catechesis of the Good Shepherd.

Jerome Berryman is a representative of the fourth generation. His work is an effort not to reproduce but to carry forward the work of his teacher, Sofia Cavalletti.

**Open classroom**—is a kind of education that is "open" in at least two ways. First, the access to the learning materials is open. Second, children can choose the means and route to achieve the agreed on learning goals.

This enables children of different learning styles and different personalities to work toward their own learning in their own way. The goal is the same for the whole class, but the way to get there is open.

**The storyteller**—is the teacher who sits in the circle with the children and presents the lesson. He or she anchors the circle and is there to greet the children when they come in and say good-bye to them when they leave.

**The teacher**—is someone, whether a storyteller or doorperson, who creates space for each child's spiritual quest and the working together of the group. He or she reaches out to all in a way that does not impose or overwhelm the children's initiative. The teacher's presence radiates respect, warmth, openness, generosity of soul, exuberance for being, curiosity, collaboration, self-discipline, and a yearning to explore. This is intentionally a poetic statement of the teacher's attitude, because it is meant to include the whole person rather than limiting the definition to how a teacher meets behavioral objectives confined to the cognition of the natural world.

The approach of Godly Play recommends that there be two teachers in each room and that one be male and the other female. Children need to see men and women in open, creative, and mutually supportive and respecting relationships.

The two teachers in a Godly Play classroom are the "storyteller" and the "doorperson". We have not found the right term for the person who sits by the door, because that person does many additional things as you will see from the book. These two roles are equal. The storyteller, however, does provide the leadership in the circle.

**A work day**—is when there is no lesson. During the typical Sunday morning there often is not enough time for the children to make an art response or get out other materials. That is fine. After several Sundays omit the lesson and go immediately to the work period. Children will remember previous lessons, personal issues they want to work on, or they will have something already in process from other Sundays. Another time that is good for a work day is when the storyteller feels uncomfortable with the lesson for the day.

11

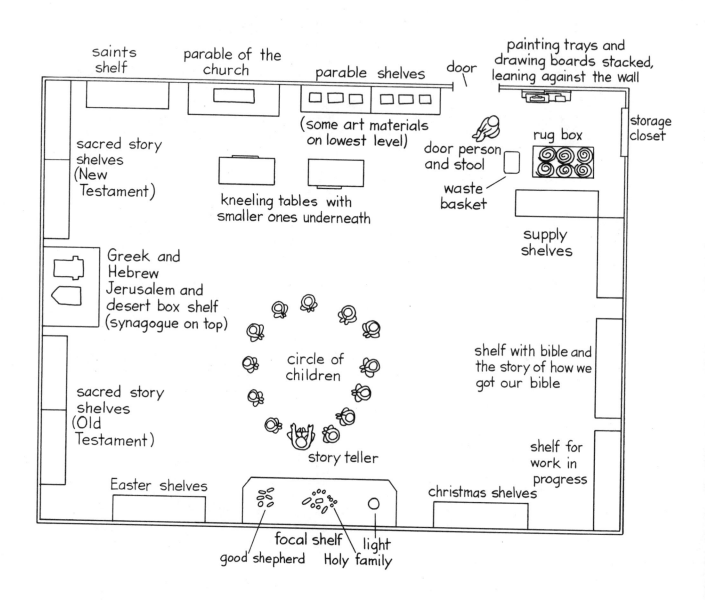

saints shelf

parable of the church

parable shelves

door

painting trays and drawing boards stacked, leaning against the wall

sacred story shelves (New Testament)

(some art materials on lowest level)

door person and stool

waste basket

rug box

storage closet

supply shelves

kneeling tables with smaller ones underneath

Greek and Hebrew Jerusalem and desert box shelf (synagogue on top)

circle of children

shelf with bible and the story of how we got our bible

sacred story shelves (Old Testament)

story teller

shelf for work in progress

Easter shelves

christmas shelves

focal shelf

light

good shepherd

Holy family

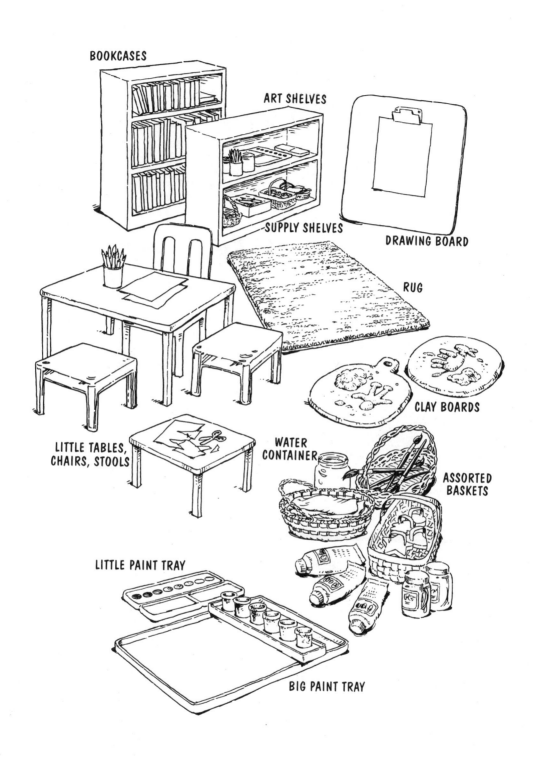

BOOKCASES

ART SHELVES

SUPPLY SHELVES

DRAWING BOARD

RUG

CLAY BOARDS

LITTLE TABLES, CHAIRS, STOOLS

WATER CONTAINER

ASSORTED BASKETS

LITTLE PAINT TRAY

BIG PAINT TRAY

# 123 Getting Started

Many adults today call themselves "spiritual," but they quickly assure themselves and others that this does not mean that they are "religious." Why not? What makes organized religion seem so irrelevant to their spiritual quest?

If we listen carefully to children and/or our own memories of childhood, we may faintly hear the beginning of an answer. The distinction is implicit in childhood. Some children already sense a difference between a nameless Power that they experience and the "Church God."

This book is the result of a lifetime of being puzzled by the distinction between God and the Church God. It is an effort to see if more can be done during childhood to bring the language and practice of the church together with the child's experience of the living God and the adult's quest to recover that kind of knowledge in an adult but childlike way.

## God and the "Church God"

The distinction between God and the Church God became clear when I read Edward Robinson's *Original Vision*. It was published in 1977 by what was then called The Religious Experience Research Unit at Manchester College, Oxford. Sir Alister Hardy, a distinguished English biologist, had asked people to write to the Unit if they had "felt that their lives had in any way been affected by some power beyond themselves." Some 15 percent of the 4,000 first responses were about experiences going back, sometimes over fifty years, to things that had happened during childhood.

15

One of the chapters in *The Original Vision* was called "Church God." It was a study of the responses having to do with the experience of God, or the lack of that experience, in churches. Both positive and negative experiences were included. The distinction, however, was much broader than that one chapter. It ran through all the accounts, because many more experiences were located outside of church than within its language and practice.

In my own life I remember being about five years old and staying with my grandmother. I cried out in the night, "I don't want to die!" Her presence in the dark helped put me in touch with a larger presence, the Power without a name, that enabled me to relax and go to sleep.

About the same time, I came home from Sunday school and proudly announced that "He eats carrots for me." I vaguely understood this was something about Jesus. I hated carrots and Jesus did hard things for people. Then I was told that I had made a mistake. The sentence I was supposed to have memorized was, "He careth for me." That was not understandable or impressive, so I lost interest.

One Easter, probably when I was in the first grade, I remember standing in the family garden with aunts, uncles, cousins, Grandmother, Mom, Dad, and some friends. We were looking at little rows of green sprouts coming up through the warming Kansas soil. I can still smell the earth, feel the stirring of warm spring winds, see the new growth, and feel the family around me. An intuition, barely formed in words, rooted itself in my memory. This awareness was something like what we had been talking and singing about in church that morning. I never told anyone about this until now. There never seemed to be the right time or place to put it into words.

When I was in the fourth grade, something happened that kept the door open for a connection between the nameless Power and the Church God. Two friends and I were very disruptive in the choir during church. The choirmaster brought the choir back after church and sat us all down.

"You boys don't have any right to destroy this. I come here to find God in the scriptures and in the singing. Your noise and disrespect stopped me from doing that this morning. You owe me and all of us an apology."

I am not sure about the words, but I can still see the traces of tears on the choirmaster's cheeks. I had thought that church didn't really matter to anyone. It seemed to be something that people just did. Now I was not so sure. The door remained open, and it still does.

The Church God is one we are told about. We are told that this God is powerful. We are told how to think and feel about this God. We are given a "mask of God" to know.

God's mask is important. We can be overwhelmed by the limitlessness of God. On the other hand, when God is given a mask to "protect" children we make a mistake. The children already know the terror in the night and joy beyond words. They cry out already to the God who has no name. A mask held in place by being polite, being quiet, never asking questions, and always saying the right words can block the experience of God.

This book is about a way that children can learn the art of how to use religious language to know God and find direction in their lives while they are still young. This book is about a possible answer to the question: "How do we teach children that God and the Church God can be the same?"

# Godly Play: A Way of Religious Education

My 1991 book *Godly Play* provided an introduction to the approach to religious education that I like to use with children (and adults). I first began to work on this with full awareness and intention in 1972 when I graduated from the Center for Advanced Montessori Studies in Bergamo, Italy. I was already trained in theology and law by that time.

The goal of Godly Play is to teach children the art of using the language of the Christian tradition to encounter God and find direction for their lives. There are six objectives that help to meet that goal.

1. To model how to wonder in religious education, so children can "enter" religious language rather than merely repeating it or talking about it.
2. To show children how to create meaning with the language of the Christian tradition and how this can involve them in the experience of the Creator.
3. To show children how to choose their own work, so they can confront their own existential limits and depth issues rather than work on other kinds of problems dictated by others, including adults.
4. To organize the educational time to follow the pattern of worship that the Christian tradition has found to be the best way to be with God in community.
5. To show children how to work together as a community by supporting and respecting each other and one another's quest.
6. To organize the educational space so that the whole system of Christian language is present in the room, so children can literally walk into that language domain when they enter the room and can begin to make connections among its various parts as they work with the lesson of the day and their responses in art or other lessons.

The activity of the teachers might be organized around two triangles formed from these objectives. One triangle is the "spoken lesson" and the other one is the "unspoken lesson." The spoken lesson involves the storyteller in wonder, the creative process, and the willingness to allow his or her existential limits into consciousness. Existential limits are such parts of life as our need for meaning, our personal death, the threat of freedom, and our fundamental aloneness. These are the boundaries that mark us as human beings. They define our existence.

Children can sense when wonder is in the air. When the storyteller wonders and is involved in discovering new and fundamental things about life, the children begin to play. Play is the way children learn how to do things, from the use of language to opening and closing doors. They will also play the ultimate game of knowing when they sense that they are in a safe place and have the appropriate tools and both the competence and permission to use them.

The unspoken lesson involves the structuring of time, the community of children, and the arrangement of the room. The longest chapter in *Teaching Godly Play* is about the unspoken lesson, because so much of the teaching is indirect and takes place through the organization of time, the support of the community of children, and the way the environment is laid out.

The time for Godly Play is organized to follow the pattern used in worship. The classical shape of the Holy Eucharist is to enter, get ready, listen to God's Word, respond, prepare for the feast, share the feast, receive a blessing, and go out. The educational setting is not the Holy Eucharist. It usually takes place when the larger church community is present. What happens in a Godly Play center is an *indirect* preparation for that form of communication, but it is still real. The reality of it rests in the unspoken but implied lesson waiting to be discovered by the children.

Structuring the community of children has to do with values. Children are given choices to make from among constructive alternatives. Sometimes children do not know how to make good choices, or cannot make them for some reason. Often they need a lot of careful and caring support.

The structure of the environment shows the children the parts of the Christian language system that includes sacred stories, parables, liturgical action, and silence. The focal point of the room is what is seen from the entryway. The Holy Family is in the center of that point of focus. The story of how the Christ Child grew up, died on the cross, and now reaches out and gives the whole world "a hug" is what it shows. Jesus is not "back then" or in "one place or another." Jesus is in all places and in all times, including the present.

On one side of the Holy Family, which represents the transformative core of the Christian tradition, is "the Light" and underneath it are lessons about baptism. On the other side is "the Good Shepherd" and underneath that are the lessons about Holy Communion. These two identity statements of Jesus and the two primary sacraments of the tradition related to them frame the Holy Family.

You may have noticed that this sounds very much like the Montessori approach to education. You are right. I have learned much from my Montessori training and years of experience as a teacher, as a teacher trainer, and as a school head.

# The Tradition of Montessori Religious Education

Maria Montessori (1870–1952) was an Italian educator who turned education upside down. She thought that if we helped children meet their needs instead of always asking them to adjust to adult needs and environments, we would see a new child, one who loves to learn. Many of the things she said shocked her contemporary educators, but today her innovations, such as little tables and chairs and manipulatives, are commonplace in both public and private schools.

In 1907 Montessori, a medical doctor, opened her first school in the San Lorenzo District of Rome. In 1910, after relinquishing her medical practice, she dedicated herself to the education of the whole child. By 1912 she was world famous and made her first speaking tour in the United States. The English version of her book *The Montessori Method,* which is still in print, was also published that year. By 1916 she had settled in Barcelona, where she remained for twenty years experimenting, training teachers, and writing.

In Barcelona she made her greatest advances in curriculum, including religious education. The demonstration school had shaded walks, a meadow, pools for fish, cages for pets, and lots of light and space in the buildings. She hired artists to make the school chapel the most beautiful space on the campus.

The children were shown how to worship by the priest that had been assigned to the school. The chapel featured child-scaled furnishings, and Montessori created additional sensorial materials about the liturgy and sacred history.

The children prepared for their first communion by harvesting the wheat, baking the bread, and marking the hosts for communion with appropriate symbols. She wrote, "The Montessori Method was furnished with a long-sought opportunity of penetrating deeper into the life of the child's soul, and of thus fulfilling its true educational mission."

During the Second World War Montessori was stranded in India and trained hundreds of Indian Montessori teachers. On Sundays she would gather a few friends and they quietly worked to perfect new religious education materials. She died in 1952 in Holland.

I am a representative of the fourth generation of this great tradition. In each generation there have been those who carefully conserved the advances of the previous generation for others to use. Godly Play is my own effort to build on the accomplishments of the previous generation.

# Getting Started

There are two extremes to getting started with Godly Play. One way is to keep doing what you are doing, but slowly implement changes in classroom management. The opposite extreme is a tremendous shock, where all of the tables and chairs are taken out of the room and replaced with shelves, little rugs and all the other Godly Play materials that the children work with.

I advise you to keep doing what you are doing and slowly integrate changes in your class. As I say this, I realize that I set up eight classrooms one summer to open in the fall at Christ Church Cathedral in Houston. Others have done this, but it is hard for people to do this so quickly. Radical change means that your efforts may attract resistance that has nothing to do with the merits of the program.

Even if you are currently using a particular curriculum, it probably will involve story-telling. One way to slowly introduce some of the Godly Play techniques is to move the tables and chairs back and make a circle of children in the center of the room for the storytelling.

You will need some people to help you prepare the feast at the end of the lesson, even if it is only juice and cookies. It is wonderful to have these things set up for you, since you will be busy with the children and wanting to give them your best attention.

It is very important also to have some people to begin to create sensorial materials to help you do the storytelling. Words do their work well, but physical materials can help you tell the story as you move its "pieces." Also, children of all ages can better wonder about a story if a concrete representation of it remains in the middle of the circle after it is finished. Words evaporate.

The opposite of the gradual approach to getting started is the shock treatment already mentioned. If you want to minimize the shock, it is a good idea to begin a year in advance. Spend a year training teachers, feast people, and material makers. It is fun to gather and work on the lessons without the pressure of having to be ready for the next Sunday.

Use the year for getting ready as a time to find the carpenters to create the shelves and other things out of wood. Art and cleaning supplies can be gathered. Parent education can begin, so the parents will know what is coming. The parents of the youngest children especially need to know about such a change.

There are several resources you need to be aware of. First, there is a book with lesson plans and patterns for materials available called *Young Children and Worship* by Sonja Steward and Jerome Berryman. *Godly Play* is available for the theory and other foundational concerns. You have this book about classroom management. Teaching manipulatives, new lesson plan booklets, collections of articles, videos, information about further training, a national newsletter, and other materials are also available from Godly Play Resources (1-800-445-4390). The purpose of all of this is to help support your work and make available the necessary resources. The difficulty in locating these resources sometimes prevents people from getting started.

You are now ready to begin the journey. The book will follow the sequence of a typical class. We will start by "entering" the subject matter and end by "going out" from it to reflect on what has happened I wish you well as we begin this quest to keep the door open between God and the Church God.

# Chapter 1

# Thresholds

Throughout the book, you and I will be having a conversation. We will be working together to try to discover the best way to work with children in religious education. You have asked me for my point of view. What do I do when I teach? This book will describe my actions in detail.

Your role in the conversation is to try to understand what I am saying, test it by your own experience in the classroom with children, and then agree or disagree. In this way we can advance the whole enterprise of religious education, of which we are a part, and both become better teachers.

Let me pause at once to add a word of caution. This book is addressed to people who like to teach children about the Christian approach to life. It seems to me that there may be something of value in this for people from other religious traditions. I keep talking about Christians in this book, because I aspire to be one, and that is where my own experience lies. It sounds exclusive, but I am only trying to work within my experience. Consider the Godly Play approach one that is waiting to be tested by you, for your own tradition and the language by which you create ultimate meaning. This is an approach to what is often called classroom management or discipline.

We will begin our discussion about how to work with children at the beginning with *thresholds*.

## Thresholds

A threshold is very important. It divides, but it also invites one to come through. At one time Jesus called himself a door, the way into a deeper reality. Your classroom door symbolizes the same thing. It divides the language and action of the everyday world from the language and action of the Christian people, which is clarified inside the Christian education classroom.

Outside of the classroom the language of Christian people is often heard by the children in bits and pieces only. How these words relate to one another is confused by the children, and the experience to which they point also is unclear. Inside the classroom the language is used carefully, so it will become more useful to the children.

We take great care when we build churches to be sure the language of the Christian people is given sensorial organization by the way interior elements are arranged. The windows, the carvings, the metal work, the colors, the type of cloth that is used, the formality of the vestments and the vessels used for Holy Communion and other sacraments, and even the shape of the church structure give the children hints about the larger reality of which these symbols are a part.

During the church service the children are not always comfortable, so it is difficult for them to relax and enjoy learning the language they hear used. Moreover, the symbols are often not explained or used in a way that is easily understood by them.

The church school and the church both use and teach the kind of communication we call worship. However, in the church school we need to be more intentional about making worship clear to the children. We want them to begin learning this powerful language by using it.

The significance of thresholds is marked in church buildings by the front steps, special carvings made of wood or stone around the door, a tower above the entrance, and in other ways. When people enter, they move from the ordinary world into a place where reflection on the limitations of our everyday language and action takes place. During worship, people use a different method of knowing to discover the ultimate meaning and direction for their lives. In the church school classroom, we are intentional about what we show the children about this special kind of communication. The doorway marks the place where one begins to *get ready*.

The teachers are the first people to pass through the door. When they enter the room, it is time to leave any biological, psychological, social, and spiritual baggage behind that is not needed when working with children. When I go through the doorway into a church school classroom the rest of the world fades away. It is time to focus on the children, their needs, and the mystery of the presence of God.

The classroom is the place for us to participate with the children in the quest for the larger reality Jesus called the Kingdom. We show the children through our words and actions, as best we can, how this journey is begun and sustained.

The growth of the community of children is guided best by having **two** teachers in the room with the children. In fact, I will use a two co-teacher model to illustrate the Godly Play approach to classroom leadership.

More than two teachers in the classroom, "over-adults" the room. The adults in the room become too obvious and reduce the consciousness of the children about their own community. The community of children is fundamentally important to the process of education that I am suggesting.

# Co-teachers and Their Roles

Each co-teacher has a specific role in the classroom. One of the adults is the *storyteller*. This person sits at the focal point of the room, where he or she can be seen easily from the doorway. This position is critical because it anchors the circle of children, and is the place where the storyteller presents "the lesson."

The role of the other adult is harder to name because of the many duties this role encompasses. Although positioned primarily beside the door, this person's role in the classroom is vital in allowing the community of children to maintain itself. This co-teacher is *the doorperson* who sits by the door and:

- *greets the children to help them get ready to enter the room when they arrive.*
- *helps the children "help themselves" get out their response work after the lesson when they are dismissed from the circle.*
- *helps the children prepare the feast.*
- *calls the names of the children who are ready to say good-bye at the end of the class.*
- *maintains the threshold and interprets what is happening inside the room to parents waiting outside.*

The storyteller and the doorperson are clearly co-teachers. This is not a situation where there is a lead teacher and an assistant. No hierarchy is involved. The tasks associated with each role illustrate the balance between the two teachers. When you experience such teaching you will discover how true this is.

# Children and the Threshold

## Helpful Hint:

What does the doorperson actually do and say? It might go something like this: "Hi, Bobby. You are the first one here. It looks like you have been running really fast. Please stand here beside me for a minute or two. That was exciting, but now it is time to get ready. Let's visit while you are slowing down." Then begin talking with the child about as many calm things that come to mind as possible.

The first person the child meets as he or she enters the room is the doorperson. It is this person's initial task to help each child get ready to enter the room. Most of the problems that arise, which we sometimes label as discipline problems or disruptive behavior, can be avoided by guiding what happens at the door.

When I first arrived at Christ Church Cathedral in downtown Houston as a consultant in 1984, the children had developed their own tradition of racing to class following the nine o'clock liturgy. The race course passed through the kitchen where the children would pause to grab a few bags of sugar to eat on the way. By the time they arrived at the door of their classrooms, their hearts were pounding wildly, their brows were moist from perspiration and they were shouting and pushing one another.

When the children were allowed to enter their rooms in this agitated state, the spirit and content of the communication to be used in the room was set by them. No matter what the adults said, the tone was about their competition, the pounding excitement they felt, and the thrill of the race. This was hard for both the teachers and the children who had not been part of the race to overcome. It was especially hard for the racers to overcome, even when they wanted to.

Sometimes children are set up for misbehavior and failure. One way to set them up for deep concentration and success, using the Godly Play method, is for the adults to be in their appropriate places before the children arrive. The person by the door might even have to pull his or her little chair out into the middle of the doorway and stop the rush.

Some children arrive already prepared to come in and sit down quietly in the circle. Others cannot settle down easily, even if they have not been involved in a race to the door. If we do not give these children our special attention at the doorway we don't give them a fair chance to take part in the community of children.

You also speak to the others who have come running up with Bobby with phrases such as, "How are you? Take your time. We have all the time we need."

While you are visiting, another child might come up slowly with his mother or father or an older brother or sister. This child is clearly ready, so he or she is greeted and invited to go on in.

The children often come in mixed bunches, which tests the calm and carefulness that the co-teacher needs to take with each child as he or she enters.

Don't hurry. Greet each one. Invite them to walk slowly into the room and sit in the circle when they are ready. Say something like: "The storyteller will help you find a place that is just right for you."

If a child is having a hard time getting ready, then keep him or her with you by the door. Keep talking with that child. Maybe he or she needs to sit on your lap for a moment. It is not fair to the community or the child to send someone who is not ready into the circle.

These alternatives will help a child find his or her own sense of self, and, on his or her own terms and at his or her own pace, discover a sense of beginning (or beginning again) competence about being in the classroom.

When a child who is being nurtured at the door settles down, he or she is invited by the doorperson to go slowly across the room and join the others in the circle for the lesson. Some children will need to stay by the door during the lesson. Tell them to find a place on the floor near you where they can see and hear. "Now, listen carefully," you might say and place a reassuring hand on the child's shoulder.

When children are sitting on the floor, the position for being ready is to sit cross-

## Helping Children Get Ready to Participate in the Community

*These actions are not required, sequenced steps to be followed like the directions in a recipe for baking a cake. Each child is different, and may not need to be taken through the entire process.*

1. *Begin by turning the child toward you. He or she may even need to cry for a little while. Hold the little one in your lap, turned toward you, and rub the child's back if he or she will allow that.*
2. *Gradually turn the child, when you can, so that he or she is sitting sideways on your lap.*
3. *Turn the child so he or she can see the other children in the circle. The child might want to turn back to the original position, if so, wait again until you think the child is ready to face this new situation.*
4. *Gradually move the child from your lap to a place on the floor beside you. Place your hand on the child's shoulder for reassurance.*
5. *Gently remove your hand from the child's shoulder when you can.*

legged with hands folded, resting on their ankles. This helps the children know where their hands and feet are. It gives them a stable center from which to pay attention.

When a child remains by the door during the lesson, he or she also stays there during the group wondering which follows the lesson. Children by the door sometimes want to join in, but they need to keep their wondering for later. Say something like, "Not now. When the lesson is over and the other children go to get their work, that will be your time to go to the storyteller and wonder about the lesson. Now it is time to listen. You are doing a good job, too. It is not always easy to get ready. That's the way. Good."

Being by the door is not a punishment. It is a way to help children learn to be ready to participate in the presentation. This is one of the most important things to learn about how the Christian language works. If you are not ready, then it is very difficult to enter the language. If you cannot enter the language, then it cannot help you discover the presence of the mystery of God.

After the children are dismissed from the circle, the child or children by the door go to the storyteller and share their wondering questions. The storyteller is always ready to listen carefully not only because these children deserve the same effort and attention as the other children, but also out of general respect for each child and his or her spiritual journey. The children who have trouble getting ready may also have the most profound things to share when you wonder together about the lesson. They have discovered them the hard way.

I marvel at how difficult it is for some children to be able to focus. It is always an honor for me to watch, support, and help guide them in their effort.

# Leaving Parents at the Threshold

The parents also are part of a child's threshold experience. The parents' needs at this leave-taking are as important as the child's, and the doorperson must keep this in mind as well.

Parents come to the doorway with many deep and mixed feelings. Some of these feelings depend on the age of the child but many parents are giving you not only their children but their *dreams* for their children. They do this with some anxiety, for what goes on inside the classroom is mostly unknown, and they are uncertain as to how their child will react to what happens there.

Some parents, of course, are relieved to hand over their children. They walk their children to the classroom with some impatience. After all, they have a class of their own to attend! At other times, regretfully, parents are going to church and leaving their children behind.

The doorway is the place for a variety of separations. The adults need to be left behind on the threshold, so the community of children has a better chance to form inside the room. This community is hardly visible when there are adults standing or sitting around the classroom.

Parents waiting inside the classroom until their children are ready to let them go, slow down the process of building up the sense of competence for all of the children in the room. This is why the doorperson needs to be firm about keeping the parents at the doorway. When there is an exception to this rule, it is usually for the extreme need of the *parent* to remain, rather than a child's difficulty in dealing with the parent's leaving.

At the doorway, the co-teacher looks at each child and says, "Good morning. I'm glad to see you."

If the parent is having trouble leaving, you might say, "Here, let me take him. That's okay. You can say good-bye at the door. No, I don't think you need to come in. No. You stay there. I will hold him for a moment. Don't worry. He looks almost ready now. Go on. I'll come get you if there is a problem. It's okay. We do this every Sunday. Now, tell Billy that you will see him after class. Say good-bye. Good. Thank you. Good-bye. We are fine."

Sometimes, parents stand outside and peer through the window into the classroom. This may be good for the parent, but is not best for the child.

The doorperson might further support parents by saying, "I know this is hard. I remember. Sometimes there are tears. That's okay. They will stop soon. We both know everything is fine, but it is still hard. If you want to wait outside to see if everything is okay, that is all right, but don't let Nancy see you. That wouldn't be fair."

When you hear crying from another room or if someone is crying in your room, it is good to acknowledge it rather than try to pretend that it is not going on. You can say things like this to the children: "Johnny is having a hard time saying good-bye today. Sometimes it is hard. He is doing the best he can." Of course, you don't want to overdo this. Especially with the young children sympathetic tears may appear and quickly spread.

After most of the children have arrived, the doorperson can step out into the hall and speak to the parents still remaining. Sometimes there are tears in the parents' eyes, too.

---

## Parents and Godly Play

*To help the parents learn about Godly Play, it is important to invite them each year at an early point in the program to a model class session. This helps calm anxiety about the unknown. Structure the class for the parents exactly as you would for the children. Don't ask them to play the role of children. Ask them to be themselves.*

1. *Have each parent get little chairs as they enter the room, or they may choose to sit on the floor.*
2. *Place the chairs in a circle in the spot where the children make their circle.*
3. *Explain the process of getting ready, and how the children enter the room.*
4. *Present a lesson.*
5. *Choose three parents to help serve the feast.*
6. *Say prayers and visit.*
7. *Show the way to say good-bye.*

---

If the parents' model class is held during the regular Sunday school hour, end the class a few minutes early to allow parents ample time to pick up their children. This is a lot to accomplish in a short period of time, but parents need to know how much is going on during the Sunday school hour.

## Showing the Community

Parents need special help to understand why they are not allowed inside the classroom. They enjoy looking around the classroom, and showing how much they support their child and the program. Often, it is difficult for them to realize how the community of children is formed until they think about and understand the process. Your job is to help them become aware of this process.

I like to use a game that is both entertaining and insightful to teach parents about the community of children. The game also illustrates why only two adults are needed in the room, and why these adults are always either seated on the floor or on little chairs.

Ask the parents to divide themselves into groups of two. Ask the "One's" to stand on a chair and talk to the "Two's." Set a time limit. Often thirty seconds is enough. Later, ask the "Two's" to stand on the chairs, and repeat the game.

When the game begins there will be nervous laughter at first, and then the laughter will turn to awareness as the parents realize that size makes an enormous difference to people. Inevitably, the person standing on the chair will start to wag his or her finger and "tell" the other person, who is now so small and lowly, what to do. Adults become instant "experts" just by being taller.

Those parents standing on the floor suddenly become inferior. This is the reason we stay down at the child's level in the classroom. We want the child to feel competent and able to make his or her own discoveries, rather than rely on a tall adult expert to tell him or her how to think and feel.

There is even a biological dimension to communication with children that can be discovered by this exercise. The person standing on the floor and looking up soon notices that the constant need to look up begins to hurt the back of the neck. Adults who remain at the child's eye level reduce this painful situation for children, which can sometimes become an impediment to adult-child communication.

Parents can also experience during the exercise that by making a special effort to communicate on their level with someone who is smaller, they are showing that person that you take them seriously. It is a mark of respect.

Once parents realize some of these things, the strange practice of asking them to stay at the door makes more sense. Adult teachers who stay below an invisible ceiling in the room will also have more confidence. Much of the teaching that goes on in the Godly Play classroom is through the community of children, so it is critical to nourish the integrity of the group.

# Starting and Ending the Class

Teachers cannot control when parents bring their children to class. The children cannot control their arrival time either. They are dependent on their elders for transportation. This means that we do not want to make the children feel bad about being late or having to leave early. Talk directly with the parents about this, instead of trying to work through the children.

The parents need to feel that the class is valuable. Perhaps their own Sunday school experience was not significant in their lives. "What difference does being on time make," they think. "Nothing is going on anyway." Helping parents value what goes on in Sunday school is a matter of education and reputation. Both take time to establish. The punctual beginning and ending of class takes careful management.

Make sure that parents know when Sunday school begins and ends. Publish it in as many places as possible. Let them know in every way possible that you think this is important and why. The choice will still be theirs. The only thing you can control is beginning and ending the class on time, with the children who are present.

When it is time for class to begin, the doorperson should close the door. Leave the door slightly ajar so that the children who arrive late can be seen. When children come to the door open it slightly and invite them to come inside. Thank the parents for bringing the child as you would any of the parents, whether the child is late or on time.

If the lesson has not yet begun, the children who are late can go one at a time to join those in the circle. If the lesson has begun, they need to stay with you by the door. Early in the lesson quietly close the door all the way.

At the end of the class open the door on time. There will be anxious parents waiting. Often they are in a hurry to go to the shore, the lake, the farm, the ranch, a restaurant, to church, or elsewhere. Some parents will recognize that you value the short time you have to keep the story of the Christian people alive. Others will see you and the children as slowing them down. When you open the door and see the parents, begin to call the names of the children whose parents are waiting.

A final related matter is the fire drill. Teachers need to know what they are going to do if there is a fire. It is astonishing how many Sunday schools are in basements or in other settings that can become firetraps. The greatest danger is being overcome by smoke during the evacuation, even if you are not trapped by flames. A good route that leads outside needs to be understood by everyone, including the parents, who will need to know where to find their children in an emergency.

Practice what to do in emergencies such as fires. These drills will also help the children know what to do. We need to practice, so we will know how to account for the children. There are many questions that need to be answered *before* a crisis occurs. The answers to these questions will help teachers and children be efficient and comfortable in dealing with an emergency.

---

 **Emergency Checklist**

✓ *Who will guide the children out?*
✓ *Who will be responsible for children who may be in the bathroom or getting supplies outside of the classroom?*
✓ *Where will you assemble outside of the building?*
✓ *Where will parents come to find their children?*

---

All of this detail is additional evidence of your respect for the children and their families. It is another way to show how Christian people live together.

We turn now to what happens after the children enter the classroom. They cross the threshold and move toward the circle. How does one build the circle and maintain it during the lesson? This discussion is valuable not only for the Sunday school "hour" but also for other times when children gather in the life of the parish. Circles and their support can work anywhere.

# Chapter 2

## The Circle and Lessons

Circles are a fundamental symbol. Their infinite number of sides, or lack of sides, provoke a sense of mystery and completeness. The Native Americans of the plains lived in circular tepees around a circular fire. To illustrate the importance of circles in their culture, an old photograph, taken at the turn of the century, shows a large group of Native Americans waiting for supplies to be handed out on a reservation. They are not in a line, but in a circle.

Circles are featured in ancient cave paintings, and are found carved on the standing stones where early people worshiped. Sometimes even the stones themselves were set in circles, perhaps marking seasonal events that corresponded with the sun and moon.

Circles articulate the sky as an upturned bowl. They show how we stand in the middle of a circle peering at the circumference of our horizon. Circles never end if your journey moves around their shape. Seasons circle about us.

The cup and the sacred vessel are also circles of power. The Greeks had their Krater or cup which stood for the matrix of creation, the divine mixing bowl into which the deity poured the elements of life. The Celtic races had their Cauldron, a mixing bowl for Rebirth, Inspiration or Plenty. The quest for the Holy Grail began with the Round Table at Camelot and ended with a circle, the chalice of healing and life. Christian baptisms are often performed using a stone circle of life-giving water.

Much can be said about the importance of sitting in circles. Sitting around a campfire on a cold evening in the forest, on the still prairie under the stars, or by moving water listening to stories stimulates ancient memories. It should. This was the method used to pass down history and stories from generation to generation. Even though most people

31

no longer sit around fires and tell stories, many of these ancient stories continue to shape our present identities.

In the church school, when we sit with the children in a circle, we too are invoking ancient memories. The themes of scripture become present to us today.

It is a good idea to place something in the center of the circle to show what the lesson is for that day. The sacred story, the parable, the liturgical event to be shown, and even silence all need a marker to help one focus. Putting the "lesson" in the center also shows that we are all the same distance from ultimate truth. It is beyond and yet near all of us, and it is the common property of everyone in the circle.

All in the circle, including the storyteller, come to the lesson equally in need to enter it. The storyteller presents the story or the parable, or demonstrates the liturgical action, but the most important part of this "telling" and "showing" is to model for the children how to enter the language of the lesson.

The language of the Christian tradition is not the storyteller's private property. His or her particular view is not necessarily the one that may hold meaning for the children. They need to find their own meaning. Sometimes, in fact, the storyteller learns from the children as they quest together to discover the presence of the mystery of God in their midst and what God would have them do and be in their lives.

# Building the Circle

When the children come into the room they move one by one to the circle as described in chapter 1. The "circle" is sometimes marked on the floor with tape, but that often gets in the way when the size of the circle needs to be adjusted. Of course, everyone can move in or back from the circle marked with tape, but my personal goal is to dispense with the tape. I like for the children to be conscious of the *circle of children* rather than the circle of tape.

As a child comes into the circle the storyteller greets the child. "Good morning. Here is a good place for you to sit." Pat your hand on the floor if the spot is near you or point if it is not. Most of the time children will merely sit down. At other times you may hear the child say something like, "But I want to sit by Bobby."

If your indication of the place for a child to sit in the circle is contradicted, you might say something like this: "If you sit here it will be easier for you to get ready."

"Let me sit by Bobby," the child holds his or her ground.

"You may sit here or go back and sit by the doorperson. You can see and hear everything from there, you know, and it will be easier for you to get ready if you sit here or there."

Flexibility is useful, but so is giving children a choice between two actions that are both good for them. Godly Play is not a method that allows the child to do anything. That attitude does not support the child. Children need limits. You need to set limits early and clearly, but you are also giving the child choices to do constructive things within those limits.

The reason for all of this talk about how to help children find a good place to sit in the circle is so they won't wind up in combinations where they stimulate each other to disturb other children, and undermine the lesson. It only takes a few weeks to know which children can work together well and which ones cannot. Our goal is to help them fit together to create a community of children where each person takes responsibility for his or her own good behavior. Then they are able to help each other enter the lesson that is presented.

While the children are coming in, the storyteller visits with the children who are already

**Helpful Hint:**

Remember that if you put a child who has trouble getting ready beside you, it is hard for you to see that child. When they are beside you it is possible sometimes to pat them or speak to them quietly. This gives these children some additional support, so they can better participate in the lesson. However, the problem with this plan is that the child might begin to present a less constructive lesson than yours during the one you are showing the children. Unfortunately, this does not become apparent until you notice the children paying more attention to the alternative lesson than to the principal one.

One of the important things about the children who are natural and creative leaders is that you want to find constructive ways to support their gifts. This means that you don't want to set up the circle in a way that you have to get into a power struggle with them every Sunday.

in the circle. Talk about school. What about the new teachers? Have they made some new friends? How are their pets doing at home? Where did they go on vacation? What was fun? What was not? There are many things to talk about.

When it is time to begin the lesson you might say, "We all need to get ready. It is time for the lesson. Everyone fix your legs and hands. Good. You know how to do this."

The children sit cross-legged with their hands on their ankles. It is not good for anyone to sit for prolonged periods in such a position, so some moving about needs to be allowed. This is, however, the position that you come back to when you need to reestablish the children's concentration by *getting ready*.

# The Presentation

We are accustomed to thinking of teaching as a transfer of knowledge. Concepts move from the teacher, who knows, to the child, who does not know. When the child can repeat what the teacher has said or written then the act of teaching/learning is completed. The teacher feels good, because the curriculum's content is remembered. The student feels good, because the teacher is the one who controls the rewards.

The Godly Play approach is different. The sacred story, parable, liturgical action, or profound silence is entered into by the storyteller in an authentic way, but the meaning gained by the storyteller is not what is shown to the children. It is the act of making meaning that is shown. The storyteller invites the student into the language of the Christian tradition by example, and shows how to become involved.

Teachers tend to teach the way they were taught, so it is difficult *not* to try to transfer concepts you have in your mind to the minds of the children. However, teaching the Christian tradition is not like teaching two plus two equals four. It is not like getting children to memorize the three main products of a state, to be written into a workbook or repeated on a test from memory. By using the Godly Play method of teaching, the storyteller shows the children the art of how to use religious language to make meaning, and perhaps even encounter the mystery of God's presence as a depth dimension in that meaning.

Inviting the children to enter the lessons and discover for themselves what the lessons mean, is existential teaching/learning. This type of learning teaches children how to use the appropriate tools to discover personal direction and meaning in life and death. It provides a theology to live and die by that continues to develop as the child does.

Some curricula in both secular and religious education require that children learn certain concepts, that specialists such as professors of education or theology, or groups such as boards of education or denominational representatives have determined are necessary, before they are considered members of a particular tradition or faith. Other experts have determined, by various means, such as developmental psychology or revelation, what children should know at different stages of their lives.

When one applies the traditional transfer model of education to the sacred stories, parables, the silence, and liturgy of the Christian people they are transformed into illustrations for concepts determined in advance by the experts. This means that when a sacred story, silence, parable, or liturgical act is introduced, its usefulness and meaning is predetermined by the conceptual limitations already decided on by the experts. This results in the minimizing of the creative and existential dimensions of the work of the Holy Spirit.

Once a concept is transferred to a child and feedback is secured about the transfer, the sacred story, silence, parable, or liturgical act is no longer important for the child to use. The illustration is no longer needed after the point is made. Yet, there is more to scripture and liturgy than the work of illustrating or ornamenting concepts. When one becomes involved in the scripture or liturgy, the Holy Spirit might take us anywhere that is relevant to who we are and our situation.

You may say that this going "anywhere" is dangerous and I agree. The control, however, is not so much in the hands of the teacher, but in the scriptures and the liturgy that have been fashioned over centuries to give an appropriate context in which one works out Christian meaning.

Like adults, children are aware of existential limits to their lives. They are able to express this in their own way, but sometimes lack both the means and the permission to do so. This is why it is so important for us to give them the language of religion. They need this collection of tools to express their deep anxiety, and to discover a personal relationship with the Creator that can help them develop in a more integrated way despite their natural limits.

Coming to grips with one's own limitations is a continuing experience. It is not a problem that can be solved by simple answers designed to fill in the blanks in a workbook, or be matched to a key of right answers. It takes entering into the creative process of existential development, where we participate with God. Godly Play is about this kind of cognition, and is *not* limited to what we have learned about the way children understand the natural world in developmental psychology.

When a Godly Play lesson is provided for children, sensorial materials are used which represent the sacred stories, parables, and liturgical action of the Christian people. There is a comfort with and incorporation of deep silence. This is so children can grasp the sacred stories, parables, and liturgical action with their senses and spirits first. Later, they will grasp the art of how to use these materials with their minds.

## ☞ Helpful Hint:

No matter what curriculum you are using, begin to collect sensorial materials on your own to accompany your presentation of the lessons. Most curricula involve the teacher in storytelling. Use the concepts suggested by your present curriculum, but when there is time learn how to use concrete materials and add them to your presentation and the environment in which you teach.

Examples of the kind of materials mentioned above are parables in gold boxes, or sacred stories on trays that hold the story pieces ready to be "told." Children of all ages need such sensorial objects to help them focus. These tangible objects also help make the storyteller a better teller of the tale and keeper of the liturgical tradition.

A storyteller who uses concrete materials in telling the story does not need to memorize the lesson. It is the moving of the pieces of the lesson that is important. This allows the story to tell itself, and the words follow.

The attitude and language that the storyteller uses to tell the story is individual, and needs to come from the storyteller's own relationship with the material. This human and spoken quality in the communication keeps the existential context present even in the silences. The unspoken valuing in the lesson is personal and alive as it flows through the relationships in the community of children and the environment of the room. This is important, because one's encounter with the existential limits to all life is very, very personal.

Good storytelling material evokes the heart of the subject matter. If the heart of the metaphor in the sacred story, parable, or liturgical act has been found and embodied by the material, then it will be something that is open to be worked with by all ages and stages of faith development. Everyone can relate to universal themes because they are so fundamental. The developmental differences will appear in the responses a person makes to the theme.

When a good material is combined with an elemental form of language in the spoken part of the presentation all the people sitting around the circle, from the oldest adult to the youngest child, can become involved in the lesson. Most important, this means that the storyteller can be authentically involved in showing the children how to use this powerful language despite developmental differences from them.

As the children move the "pieces" of the sacred story, parable, or liturgical action they are creating their own meaning in the presence of God and in the community of children.

The storyteller does not tell the children how to feel and think about the presentation. This might force the children to give up their own interpretation in favor of what the teacher tells them, and lead to a false sense of their theological worth.

The goal of the Godly Play approach is for children to use religious language in an appropriate way, while they are learning what that language is about. In this way they learn by doing. The "doing" is serious, yet playful.

The playful aspect of this approach is critical. Making meaning is a kind of play. It uses the creative process that we have been given as creatures created in the image of the Creator. The deep play of children is how they learn everything that is important to them.

Children must learn all sorts of things including: how to get dressed, go to sleep, go to the bathroom, use language so others can understand them, eat in a socially appropriate manner, be away from home, miss their parents, and survive with babysitters. They learn these things by doing them. They play their way into such knowledge and their knowledge develops positively if the adults are playful too.

To learn how to use the sacred stories, parables, and liturgical acts to make existential meaning for their lives, the children need also to learn how to love this language and respect its power. The quality of the relationship with the language also must be shown.

What Paul wrote about love in 1 Corinthians 13 could be said about the quality of relationships in a game played by those who play for the pleasure and meaning of play itself. The children do this naturally face-to-face. Adults play in a mirror dimly, but they can give up *childish* ways and become like children in a second naïveté when they learn again to truly play.

# Guiding the Group Wondering

The wondering begins as the lesson comes to a close. This is guided and supported by the storyteller. While this is going on the doorperson pays attention, but does not distract by voicing his or her own wondering. That can be kept until after class. Of course, the co-teacher does not get up and dust the shelves, cut paper, or repair materials. That would be a blatant disrespect for the children and the process in which they are engaged.

Helping children wonder about the presentation is not like finding out whether they can remember what has been said. As we discussed at the beginning of this chapter, if the teacher's statements can be repeated by the children, many adults are satisfied that a transfer of knowledge has taken place. That is not what wondering entails.

Through the Godly Play approach, children are taught the ability to use the parables, sacred stories, or liturgical events which have been presented to discover and name God's presence. The knowledge of so-called "biblical facts" will follow from this use, but these conceptual bits and pieces are learned because, as tools, they are useful to the children for their own creation of existential meaning. The learning is not done to please adults but to profoundly please the children.

Not only is wondering together a guide to learning how to use religious language personally, but it is also a guide to learning the corporate use of religious language. This is an indirect preparation for active community worship in the "big church" and the ministry of the laity.

The teacher's responsibility in the group wondering is to genuinely enter the lesson himself or herself. The unspoken part of the lesson is the authentic participation of the teacher, who is moving toward discoveries appropriate to himself or herself. There is no talking down to children as they wonder, or boiling down of scripture's profound depths to a thin "kiddy religion." This kind of communication is not cute.

This interaction is seriously playful. It is serious because it gives the children something they need, a language to use to cope with their own existential issues. It is playful because children learn what attracts their interest, and helps them grow.

Religious language attracts the interest of children, once they learn to enter it, since it is so powerful. It gives them a sense of home, wherever they find themselves. This sense of home comes from the relationships they establish with their own deep selves, with others, with God, and with God's creation. It is not the surface facts of parables, silence, sacred stories, or liturgical acts that attracts them. It is the sense of presence that these types of religious language point to that calls to them. This sense of presence is the only way to transcend the existential limits to our lives.

By "existential limits," I mean the personal experience of our own death, our sense of fundamental aloneness despite community, our need for meaning, or the scary appreciation of what it means as human beings to be free. These existential issues are as fundamental to the lives of children as they are to adults. Children may experience these issues at different levels and speak of them in different ways than adults do, but they are certainly as real to them as they are to us.

For example, a young child left alone experiences the presence of all four of the existential boundaries mentioned above. They are not distinguished into four different kinds of issues, because the child does not have the ability, the language, or the permission to explore them to the point that such distinctions might be made. Nevertheless, the pressure of these absolute boundaries can be felt and our task is to give the children the means to express and cope with the anxiety this pressure causes. I propose that this is the function of religious language.

Godly Play gives the children something they deeply need, so it makes them joyful. This is not the elation that entertainment might give. It is the happiness that the satisfaction of the soul's wholeness can give.

To be more specific there are four kinds of meaning that religious language provides for children: *parables, silence, sacred stories, and liturgical acts.* Each of these subfunctions of religious language generates slightly different kinds of wondering. Silence needs silence, but the rest need language.

## Parables

Parables provoke the experience of "un-think-able thought." They encourage a paradox that pushes language to its limits. For example, parables illustrate that the kingdom of God is not something that can be expressed easily using ordinary language.

Parables turn the world of the everyday upside down, and ask us to begin anew to make sense of life without the ordinary cultural limits. Parables want us to experience life bound only by the absolute, existential limits rather than transitory ones. This is what makes studying parables such an unusual experience for adults and children who have been educated to believe that only the correct answers win favor.

The fundamental wondering question for working with parables is: "I wonder what this could really be?" In the parable of the mustard seed, for example, the storyteller might point to the birds and ask, "I wonder if the birds have names? I wonder if the birds are happy? I wonder how the birds found their way to the great shrub? I wonder how they knew where to build their nests?" The wondering can go on and on, and the direction it takes depends on the children and their needs.

"I wonder what the person who put the tiny seed in the ground was doing when the tiny seed was growing? I wonder if the person has a name? I wonder if the person can take the shrub that grew so big it was like a tree and put it back inside the tiny seed? I wonder if the person was happy to see the birds? I wonder if the person helped the birds build the nests?" It is good to stop just before the wondering begins to run out of energy. This leaves the children with a taste for more parables in a future class.

## Sacred Stories

The wondering that follows a sacred story is not about the un-think-able. It is about our deep identity. This type of wondering narrates the great story and gives our own stories context and a larger meaning.

The primary theme I use to tie together the narrative of scripture is that of the encounter of people with the elusive presence of the mystery of God. Every curriculum has some theme that is followed, whether it is explicit or not. Samuel Terrien's work, especially his book *The Elusive Presence,* is the primary source that can be used to develop this organizing theme.

The reason I like to use the experience of the elusive presence of the mystery of God as an organizing theme is because children already may have an awareness of God before they speak of it. By presenting the sacred story of encounters with God's mystery by the people of God, children are given both a language and permission to express what they have experienced and to form their identity around that experience.

It is not unreasonable to think that children experience the presence of the mystery of God. Both systematic empirical studies and anecdotal evidence, including my own research, are now available to suggest that this is true.

The wondering begins after the story is told.

## Sacred Story Wondering Questions

After the story is finished the parts of it still remain in the middle of the circle to reflect on.

1. Begin by saying, "I wonder what part of the story you like best?" This opens the possibility that children may like different parts of a sacred story. Each child is thus supported to express his or her authentic feelings about what matters to them if they so desire.

2. "I wonder what part of the story is the most important?" This question suggests a distinction between what may delight you in a peripheral way, and what you think is central. It takes both the thinking and the feeling of the children seriously.

3. "I wonder who you are in the story? I wonder what part is about you?" As you can see, this gives the child an opportunity and permission to project himself or herself more deeply into the story. This is more difficult for children in early and middle childhood than in late childhood, but such theoretical limitations should not prevent us from posing the wonder of such an important question. Even asking yourself what the *question* means is the beginning of a discovery that can satisfy you at that time in your life.

4. "I wonder if there is any part of the story we can leave out and still have the story?" This kind of wondering question reverses the known and the unknown in the story, and allows the child to express personal interests by editing the story. It also gives the storyteller a way to see if the children were able to find the central core of the story by reflection on the concrete material and the spoken lesson. This kind of wondering helps improve the language, the method used for teaching the lesson, and the teaching materials used as well as giving children another way to be involved.

I like to keep reminding the children that this is not easy. With sacred stories, parables, and the liturgy there is always more to uncover. These three cannot be worn out, and are never empty. Something new is always there waiting for us. This is true also of silence, but there is no specific material for that discovery. It is in all the materials and the relationships.

One of the primary things that is being taught here is the love of playing seriously with the sacred stories, parables, silence, and liturgical action. Even if a question does not yet make sense to a child, the love of probing reality with religious language is conveyed.

Other wondering questions about narrative can be formulated as the occasion suggests. Children will give the storyteller the lead, but as you can see, the four questions suggested above have a great deal to do with identity. They are to guide the children into a better understanding of who they are and where they are going, by showing how *their* story is a part of the great story.

## Liturgical Acts and Symbols

The third kind of wondering questions are related to lessons about liturgical action and symbols. For example, suppose the lesson is about the liturgical year. You might have a circle made of paper, cardboard, foamcore, or wood to draw the children into the meaning of this method of tracking time.

At first, this lesson appears to be one that lends itself to questions with correct answers. There are four Sundays in Advent, six Sundays in Lent, and so on. However, it is the dynamic of the year that we are after. The church keeps time in a special way. Take the whole circle of the year apart and as you put it back together again you wonder at its structure and meaning with the children.

- "I wonder which of these great times you like best."
- "I wonder how the colors make you feel."
- "I wonder what the colors make you think about."

You can see that this kind of wondering leads the children more deeply into their personal responses to the way the church keeps time. There is a second and just as important aspect to this.

This second dimension relates to the liturgy, and deals with the connection children make between what they learn in the church school and their experience of worship in church with the rest of the parish family. The wondering probes this connecting link: I wonder if you have ever come close to this color? I wonder where else you can find this color in the church? I wonder who put the color there? I wonder where the other colors are when you don't see them?

It is especially good for the young children to visit the church as part of these lessons. They need to notice, name, and value these colors and their symbolic places in relation to each other and their role in worship. The older children have had more experience in the sanctuary, and can remember more about the church context while remaining in their classrooms.

41

During their visit to the church, the children can be told the stories about the vessels, vestments, symbols, and the whole setting of the church by people who care for these items. This puts the place, the value, and the names together for the children, and gives them a concrete foundation for this kind of wondering. The wondering process remains playful and open, as well as specific and useful for the worship of the younger children.

Two final points must be made about the quality of the children's wondering. Does anything go? What kinds of responses from the storyteller are both supportive, and encourage authentic wondering?

The wondering that the children do is usually genuine. It is promoted and shown by the storyteller through genuineness in asking wondering questions. It is easier for an experienced teacher to be genuine than a new teacher because the seasonsed teacher has already experienced the children expanding upon their own previous wondering. Once new teachers experience this type of wondering and learning from the children, the draining feeling that they sometimes experience changes to a feeling of synergy with the children.

If the child's wondering is genuine, and that is always a judgment call, it is supported, no matter how strange it might seem. The "strangeness" might be from the child's inability to put the experience into words. It also might be that what the child is wondering cannot be put into words. It remains an encounter with mystery.

Misinterpretation of what a child has attempted to say is dangerous. You may be asking the child to either give up his or her interpretation of personal experience, or agreement with a trusted adult. This double bind is hard to escape, but saying something slowly and authentically like, "Hmm, I wonder," may do it. With this language the adult can join the child in the wondering and be supportive without introducing the bind or blocking the wonder.

The wondering by the group about the lesson brings us to the next step in the process of a Sunday morning church school session. It is now time for the children to be dismissed from the circle to get out their "work."

This is called "work" to give the activity a serious quality, like that given in the adult world to important activities. It is actually deep play. It is serious because it helps the child grow and become more fully integrated as a biological, psychological, social, and spiritual being.

# Working with Disruptions in the Circle

There are bound to be disruptions in the circle on some days. This is to be expected, no matter how much the children trust the storyteller and find the classroom to be a safe place. This will happen no matter how well prepared you are or how nicely the presentation is going. Disruptions are an opportunity for teaching, and are *not* always the failure of the teacher to teach well.

## Troubleshooting

Sometimes I say, "Let's make our circle a bit bigger so everyone can see." This is a little better than saying, "Everyone move back from the line about this much (showing the amount with my hands)." Some children would move all the way back to the walls in the room if possible to see what the teacher would do and to check on who makes the rules in the room. We might call this the "Changing Circle Game." The emphasis is on the community of children and not so much on the mechanics of making the circle bigger or smaller if you refrain from marking the circle on the floor with tape.

Notice that I did not say that the "Changing Circle Game" would be completely avoided by the lack of tape. Some children still love to get that going. It can get the teacher disorganized, but it is also a time when you can show the children that they can depend on you to be calmly in charge. Once they know that, the children also know they can risk expressing scary thoughts and feelings in this warm and open, yet safe and orderly, environment.

Disruptions express many things for the children. For example, disruptions help them test the safety of the place in which they find themselves. Responses by the teacher to disruptions show what the boundaries are for behavior. Children need to know if they will be safe from their own chaos, as well as that brought to the circle by other children.

Misbehavior also is a way for the children to see if the adults in the room really can work together. Somehow children seem to be born with both an interest and ability to perform "little experiments" on the adults in the classroom, to see if they can be split on a particular issue. Children like to know if they can divide and conquer the adults, and then take over the classroom.

I don't mean that they think all of this out consciously. It is not until late childhood that children actually become aware of these sociological interests and begin to conduct their experiments with full intent. Before the age of seven, children do this by intuition.

Again, the most powerful teaching is by showing, not by talking about something. You show the children that they are safe, and that there are rules. Chaos cannot prevail and lead to self-destruction or being hurt by others.

You also show that the adults in the room communicate well with each other, and that they understand children and how the class works. Each knows his or her role and is comfortable with it. Children can be shown that the adults in the room work well together, and that they cannot be split. This is not something the children need to worry about.

Each problem that is presented is a teachable moment to show how the community of children can work together as Christian people. The storyteller and the person by the door work together to help that happen.

When there is disruption in the circle, the storyteller and the co-teacher understand that there are five levels of response that can be considered. Each response involves both co-teachers.

## Five Responses to Disruptions

**First Level:** Both co-teachers check themselves to be sure that they are deeply involved in the presentation. All we can really do is show the children how to participate in the language of the Christian people. Participation is the key that opens the door into the language. It is something that will not work unless you are "inside."

Participation by the storyteller usually helps children who are easily distracted to come back and focus. The doorperson's concentration also has an impact on the whole system of relationships in the room, including the relationship between each person in the room and the lesson. Wandering attention is called back into the lesson by example.

It is more difficult to show how to "enter" the powerful language of the Christian people when you do not have the concrete materials to set in the middle of the circle. These materials give a physical focal point for the children's attention. Such things as a gold parable box, figures being moved over an underlay, or a journey being made by little stand-up figures across the sand in the desert box make this process more tangible.

Your deepening concentration shows the disruptive child that you will not support his or her misbehavior. You do not even acknowledge it. What is going on in the lesson is much more important. Since you do not reinforce the child's bid for attention, he or she sometimes will stop and begin to follow the behavior you are modeling.

Despite all attempts, there will be times when some children cannot refocus. They need help. It is not fair to the other children in the circle, who are attending to the lesson, if a disruptive child does not get the necessary help to return to being ready.

**Second Level:** Briefly look up from the lesson and say to everyone, "We need to get ready again. Watch. This is how we get ready. Okay?" As you say this, show the children how you have your legs crossed and your hands resting on your own ankles. Then look back down at the lesson you are presenting and return to your own deep concentration.

You still have not responded to the particular misbehavior of a specific child. You have resisted reinforcing it at this level as well. You also have helped the whole community refocus. This may help the misbehaving child to recognize how the rest of the community of children is working together to enter the lesson. He or she might like to join that community of interest.

As you know, it is very hard for some children to resist trying to take over the circle and become the teacher. Both power and control are at stake, so they disturb to see if the teacher really is in charge, and to see how much power they have. Often these children cannot resist the stimulus of being close to the other children without undermining what is being presented. It sometimes sounds like they want to present an alternative lesson. They want to be the teacher. There are many additional reasons—biological, psychological, social, and spiritual—why children are disruptive.

**Third Level:** The storyteller looks up and says, "No, that is not fair. Look at all of these children who are taking part in the lesson. They are ready. You need to be ready too. Let's try again. Good, that's the way." You again show all the children how to sit and how to fix their hands. You then return to the lesson.

All of these responses are neutral as far as feeling is concerned. Keep the tone of your voice and attitude as matter-of-fact as possible. Don't let the disruptive child "hook you," so that you respond with an emotional outburst or an argument. Some children are looking for this type of reaction. They may not know any other way to relate to an adult.

Remember your own school days. Even if you were not usually disruptive, there was something about a substitute teacher that could bring out the mischief in you. Children go to work on teachers who do not appear confident. Their reward for this effort is some kind of emotional outburst. Adults sometimes even flee from the room for a time. There is a lot going on in such a transaction, but what Sunday school teachers need to know is that they are viewed by school-wise children as something like a substitute teacher. Such testing by children should not be taken personally.

**Fourth Level:** Ask the child to go across the room slowly and carefully to sit by the person by the door. Do not do any explaining or reasoning with the child about this. If you have tried the first three levels of response, the child already is quite aware of what is going on. It may even be that the child would like to go sit by the door-person, so he or she can pay better attention.

This response also is done from a neutral feeling position. If you charge your words with too much feeling it shows your exasperation and gives overtones of punishment. This is not a punishment or an expression of your exasperation. It is a matter-of-fact move by a teacher to help a child be able to be ready so he or she can better attend to the lesson.

The child may buck. "Do I have to?"

"Please get up now and walk carefully to where the coteacher is and sit down. Find a place where you can see and hear. It will be easier for you to be ready if you sit by the door."

In some cases you need to move to the next level of response. The child says, "No." This brings us to level five, and the card you do not want to have to play. It is your last card.

You might say, "It is time to go *now*." This also may not be enough. "May I help you?" Do not get up to walk with the child unless you absolutely have to. By standing up, you break down the community of children by turning into a tall adult who forces children to do things, rather than someone who guides the community of children to be able to take care of itself.

> **☞ Helpful Hint:**
>
> As the storyteller works his or her way through the five levels of managing misbehavior in the circle, the door-person may begin to feel like leaving his or her chair to help. That is a mistake. This robs the situation of the distance between the child and the door-person.

It is better if the child has to walk with intention from the circle to the person by the door. As that happens, the reorganizing of the child's self-understanding has already begun. This movement with intention can help the child to begin to take responsibility for himself or herself. This makes the time by the door-person much more constructive, because it is without the stigma of having been imposed.

The distance between the circle and the door is very important for many reasons. We are not trying to tell the children how to think or feel. We are not telling them what to do. We are trying to guide them toward taking responsibility for their own actions and to learn how to participate with others in a kind of communication and lifestyle that marks the Christian people. The action cannot be forced and the language cannot be laminated on the child's consciousness by memorization like a new surface. Both must grow from a personal interaction with the environment.

In order to be useful to the child, the constructive use of the creative process needs to be internalized. If it does not become the child's own, then in a later and different life crisis the motivation will not be deep enough to withstand the tricks of reason, or the force of feelings that can carry the child into destructive behavior. We are working for the deep participation by the child in Christian values. We are not merely trying to make children be nice and quiet in Sunday school.

Being nice and being quiet are not values that will serve the child well in the existential crises in life. They need courage, a sense of who they are, and the ability to use the tools of Christian communication to find meaning in a relationship with the presence of the powerful mystery of God.

When the child must leave the circle to be better able to become ready, the storyteller goes on with the lesson, returning to deep concentration. The child moves into the sphere of the doorperson.

There are several levels of response available to the person by the door to help the child learn how to get ready and how to participate within the limits of his or her new surroundings.

Sometimes the child wants to sit in the doorperson's lap. This is usually a younger child's need, but you would be surprised at how old some children are who need the same thing. It is hard to get to church on Sunday. Who knows what has happened? Sometimes children are so pushed and rushed that their feelings of being present in their own experience do not catch up with them until after their inner chaos settles down. Perhaps, no one has had the time even to say "Good morning" to the child yet and give him or her a hug.

As mentioned in chapter 1, there are five levels of response for lap-sitting. The only difference in the process this time is that the person by the door holds out his or her hands to see if the child moves towards the lap. If that does not happen, the co-teacher motions to a place on the floor, close to his or her chair where the child can sit. In chapter 1 the issue was separating from the parents and entering the threshold of the room. Now the issue is getting ready in the circle, amid the community of children.

Should you ever remove a child from the room? It is best to manage all discipline problems in the classroom, since the removal of a child from the room signals the successful manipulation of the teacher by a child. It also shows that this is not a place with secure boundaries that will be maintained even under duress. It also shows a kind of giving up on a child, so the place may not be safe if a child is overcome by chaos. Ultimately, sending a child outside the room breaks down the community of children and shows that it cannot maintain itself even with help from trusted adult guides.

Of course, if the safety of the children is threatened by a child who is out of control, removal may be necessary. Certainly, you need immediate, competent help. The children will sense this extreme emergency when this happens. It may be that they have already become fearful that this will happen someday. They will be glad to know that you can act on their behalf quickly and with sure confidence.

Action such as restraining or removing a child still should not be allowed to look from the outside or feel from the inside like it is punitive. The child who is restrained or removed, and the watching children, need to know that sometimes people get so upset they don't know what to do. They are so confused that they can't even hear what the people who are there to help have to say.

If a child must be removed from the environment, be sure that someone is with him or her at all times. That person could be one or both of the child's parents, another volunteer who helps with the Sunday school, or even the doorperson. However, the last instance would complicate matters in the classroom.

Both parents and children need to know that you are willing to be frank and open about extreme behavior, as well as the garden variety mischief. This shows that parents and teachers are working together. Most problems are helped greatly when children realize that they cannot split teachers from each other or teachers from parents.

It is very important to involve parents in these emotional situations. This lets them know the difficulty firsthand, and that you and they need to work together to solve this problem. Sometimes a crisis must occur before a family is willing to make the needed changes in their relationships.

Unfortunately, not all parents are ready to handle such a situation. They would rather blame the teachers, the program, or the child. Whatever the reaction of the parents, the Sunday school is part of a larger system of relationships including the family, the week-day school, friends, relatives, and many others who can work for the good of the child.

If possible the child needs to continue with the lesson for the day even if he or she must leave the room. The misbehavior cannot be rewarded by allowing the child to leave the room and do what he or she wants. The child needs to know that you think that what is going on in the circle is important, so you do not want him or her to miss it. This effort will let the child know that although he or she has been removed from the community for a time, he or she is not excluded. The whole community is there for the child when he or she is able to be ready, and to cooperate with the other children to enjoy the lesson. A child who is out of control is not an outsider.

The removal of a child is an extreme and unusual situation, but we must be prepared for it. Let us now return to the normal flow of this process and take up the question of how to guide the response time of the children.

# Chapter 3

# Responses

$T$he many details involved in setting up an open access environment for learning can add up to something very important to the children. The organization of the room itself can work either for or against children when it is time to continue exploring their personal responses to the Word of God.

In this type of environment, the children get to do something that the adults in church must do silently and alone, or by whispering to a neighbor during worship. It is only later that adults can discuss with friends or family, perhaps over lunch, what they discovered while in church.

The act of worship is not complete until insights are articulated and shared. Proclamation is not one-way communication that ends with its utterance. It assumes continued rumination and expression as well as action by those who encounter God's Word. Children need to learn this by doing it.

## Getting Out Your Own Work

When the wondering of the group winds down, the storyteller invites each child, one at a time, to go get out his or her "work." I always go from my right to my left around the circle. You may decide to choose another way.

The method you choose is something that does not need to be debated each Sunday. Small issues, like this one, you can decide for the children so that the bulk of their time is left to work on major issues.

49

Sometimes the children will challenge your method, especially those who will have to wait the longest. Others will adjust themselves to your decision by sitting on the side of the circle where you always begin. Usually, however, they are not that interested and forget.

The direction we go around the circle is a custom like traffic lights that enable us to live together better. We would never get to our destinations if we had to sort out every busy intersection without traffic lights.

Something that is not purely a matter of custom, however, is that the children who are sitting on the opposite side of where you start will need to be given continual support. To help them be patient you might say, "That's the way. This is taking a long time. Be sure that you already know what work you want to get out. Do you know yet? You're doing a good job. Good, good." Sometimes only a touch, a wink, or a smile is enough to support the waiting children.

**Helpful Hint:**

Sometimes children use technical terms for the body parts they think they are not supposed to talk about, such as "penis" or "vagina." They may not even know what parts they are referring to. They have seen these words get a lively reaction from their teachers, especially in Sunday school. It is important to listen to see where they are going with this, even if we are shocked. It is almost like the children don't want to waste a good "bad word." They try the technical terms for forbidden subjects to shock you first and if that doesn't work they may move to the category of bad words like "shit" to see how that works.

Children are swamped by commercials today. Much of what is seen by children disturbs them in ways they do not have words to express. The violence, the destruction of the environment by machines, the exploitation of human beings and animals, and the sense of being controlled by something they do not understand are all issues that contribute to their need to express something that gets a dramatic response. There is much in our culture that is destructive and confusing to children. They need a safe place to sort out some of this. This is true even if they introduced the issue inappropriately.

If you do not have the time in class or the inclination to work one of these forbidden-word situations all the way through to something constructive, you can always give the child a short but good listen and then say in a neutral way, "Let's work on something else now."

Our task as teachers is to take the children seriously to see where they want to go with such words and eventually help them link their expression with the language of the Christian tradition. This approach both reduces the use of either kind of language for its shock purpose, and it sometimes leads to something serious and constructive, as in the story of Arthur later in this chapter.

As you begin to move around the circle you might say, "What work would you like to get out this morning?" Sometimes the child already has something in mind to work on. It may be related to the lesson of the day, or perhaps it is work that was unfinished on a previous Sunday. The day's work could even be something about an issue that has come up in the child's life that shows no immediate or apparent connection to the lesson or anything in the room.

It is important to give special consideration to the responses that seem to have no connection with what the class is working on. Existential issues and the mystery of the presence of God are difficult for children and adults to articulate. We need to be alert to recognize when children are trying to say something about these difficult issues.

Also included here is the factor of being defensive in order to protect oneself from being overwhelmed by the existential limits to our lives, or to the immensity of the experience of God's presence. The child may be indirect, because to be direct would sweep him or her away with emotion. On the other hand, much disconnected communication is only the meandering of a wandering mind or a knee-jerk expression of what he or she has been taught by the TV.

Using a Godly Play approach to classroom management and the learning environment can show children, using their own work, how to integrate deeply their lives and their expressions by using the language of the Christian people. For some children this takes an enormous effort as well as great skill and support from the co-teachers to discover how to do this. For other children it comes quickly and naturally.

Helping children decide something simple like what art medium he or she is to use to make a response is a first step toward the child moving with intention to express himself or herself. One way to support the child to take the next step, once a medium has been chosen, is to say things like, "That's good. Be careful now. Pay attention. I'll bet your fingers already know what you are going to make. Get everything out you need to work with and then just let them go. Do you have your fingers with you? Be sure to take them with you. I think you are already beginning."

As you go around the circle for the first time, move rather quickly so that the children who do have a project in mind can get started. If someone is taking a long time to decide, say something like, "That's okay. We'll go on. Keep thinking. I will come around again soon. That's the way. Keep thinking."

Go around the circle a second time. Help as many of those children make up their minds as you can without getting too bogged down. When you come around a third time the group should be smaller, so you can take more time with each child.

Finally, only one or two children will be left who cannot make up their minds. You might give them another lesson or repeat the one you just gave in the circle. When you are finished ask them, "Now, what work would you like to get out?" The process used with the whole circle at the beginning is now repeated with more individual attention for this small group that is left. This personal attention teaches the children many good things about how this classroom works and their ability to make it work for them.

Dismissing the children one at a time from the circle does not mean that the children only work alone. Open classrooms provide many opportunities for children to learn how to work together. Suppose Mary says, "I want to work with the Creation Material." This is a set of seven cards, one each about a day of creation.

"That would be good work, Mary. Please go and get out that good work." Mary trudges off toward the shelf that has the tray on it.

When you continue on around the circle Nancy declares that she also wants to work with the Creation Material. "That is wonderful work, Nancy, but Mary is already working with the Creation Material. Go and ask her if you can work with her. Now, remember she might say, 'No.' That's okay. Just ask her if she will come get you when she is finished, so you can work with it after she puts it away."

Sometimes children need help from the storyteller or doorperson to carry on such a conversation with another child. This kind of situation is hard to manage even for adults. No one is very comfortable asking a personal question that may have "No" for the answer. Taking such a chance is something most of us need to learn. It is something else that Christian people need to be able to do to live together well.

When children need someone to support them in such a dialogue the doorperson is typically the person to assist them. This is another reason why the doorperson needs to stay involved and alert to what is going on in the circle. When co-teachers can anticipate each other no special briefing is necessary. Everything flows smoothly.

If the child already working with a material does say "No," then the child who posed the question needs to choose another type of work until the first child is finished. That choosing may take some thinking by the child and more support from the teacher. You may need to send the child back to the circle to take another turn and listen to the other children's choices. The storyteller takes over again when the child is back in the circle.

Some of the children might choose to work with some material you have previously presented. It might be a sacred story, a parable, or something about the liturgy of your tradition. What is important to note is that children sometimes will return again to a material previously worked with regardless of the day's lesson. An extreme example of this was two boys in one of my classes who returned again and again to the Parable of the Mustard Seed over a twelve week period.

The shelves where the art materials are kept become very important to the "work" process. They are set up to give the children open access to what they need to express themselves.

# Responses and the Active Environment

## *The Art Shelves*

The art shelves are where the things are kept that the child needs for expressing himself or herself. These things, like paints and clay, are grouped so it is clear to the child how to use what is kept there.

The doorperson needs to check the art shelves before class. Are the pencils sharpened? Have the tempera paints dried up or grown moldy? Do they need to be refreshed and stirred? Is there fresh water with the watercolors? Is there enough paper? Has it been cut into large, medium, and small sizes? Is the clay sealed in the plastic containers and soft? Does it need to be rolled into small balls?

## Troubleshooting

When a trivial choice comes up you can guide the child back toward the materials you have in the classroom. We once had a child who was referred by a psychiatrist to our experimental class on Saturdays. Let's call him Arthur. One day Arthur couldn't make up his mind about what to work on, but I could get him to decide what he wanted to work with. I had set up a choice between two constructive alternatives, the watercolors and the "big paints." The big paints are the tempera colors in paint pots that are applied with large brushes. He went to work with the doorperson's help.

When Arthur told me about his painting I began, as I usually do, by making supportive but open responses to the child's work. "Hmm. Brown." I traced the brown lumps running along a line along the bottom of the page. Then I waited.

"Dinosaur bowel movements," he said seriously.

"What?" I was not sure what I had heard, but I responded with the same seriousness that he spoke with.

Arthur said, "They are dinosaur bowel movements."

"Yes." I affirmed what they were, but paused to see if he would continue. I wanted to know if he would add anything to help me see what direction he wanted to go with this.

I continued, "Yes, I can see that now. Good." I paused again to see if he would give me some direction so I could support what he needed to talk about. Finally, I decided that he was probably only trying to shock me, so I moved toward trying to connect this response with something constructive in the room from other lessons.

"Did you know that sometimes dinosaur bowel movements are still found today? They are so old they have turned to stone."

Silence.

My response and its feeling tone had shown Arthur that he could talk about anything he needed to with me in this place, but I may have missed what he wanted to talk about. I stayed alert for any further clues as I began to see if I could help him connect this to something in the room.

"They are a wonderful discovery. They turn to rock after many centuries, you know. Professors use a special saw to cut the rocks into very thin slices. They then look at the slices with a microscope to tell what the dinosaur had been eating. The discoveries have been very interesting."

There was more silence from the child, but he did seem to be listening. Still, I stayed alert to see if I was taking him away from something he wanted to talk about.

"This is good work. I wonder if there is anything in our classroom that you would like to put in your picture?"

Silence.

"Walk around the room and see if anything calls to you."

Arthur got up and began to walk around the room. He wandered a while and began to appear stuck, so I eased in beside him to see if I could get him exploring again.

"Let's go around together."

We walked around the typical Godly Play environment with sensorial materials sitting on the shelves. When we came to the sacred story shelves we began to walk along the area where the lessons about Creation, Noah and the Flood, Abraham and Sarah, The Exodus, The Ten Best Ways to Live, The Church that Was a Tent, The House for God in Jerusalem, and other lessons are kept on the top shelf. He paused as we went along, and then turned around. He went back along the shelf and stopped in front of the material for the lesson about the Creation. "Hmm. Why don't you take this material over to your work and see if there is anything that is just right for your painting?"

The material for the lesson about the Creation is a tray with a set of cards on it, one for each of the days of creation, and a rolled-up black cloth. He spread out the cloth which is the underlay and placed the seven cards on it in succession. He put the card about Day Six, the one that shows "the creatures that walk upon the earth," next to his painting and looked across the room at me. I returned to where he was working when I finished with another child. "This looks interesting. Wonderful."

He began to draw into his painting some figures from Day Six. Animals and even people began to "walk upon the earth" in his painting.

Arthur's expression in painting, whether it was of an existential issue in his life or to get my attention, was treated with respect and creative energy. This helped him bring it into conversation with the domain of religious language. It was his connection with God's creation that gave his work constructive expression. Everything in this creation is a gift from God. Even dinosaur bowel movements and the child who painted them are precious.

Soon after this Saturday Arthur began to make blue birds rather than the violent and vivid, twisting sheets of fire he usually made. The dinosaur bowel movements had been an important exception to his usual fare of fire. That was a special day. He had discovered something important, something existential that day, and he began to grow again, to heal a little more, and become a more integrated person.

The whole room needs to be checked as well. Does the carpet need to be cleaned or do the shelves need to be dusted? One of the ways children can tell if this place is important and needs to be respected is by seeing how the room and the materials are maintained.

While the doorperson is checking the room the storyteller should check the materials needed for the lesson of the day. For example, suppose you have parables in gold boxes in your room. They need to be checked to see if the objects to be placed on the underlay are all there and in good repair. Is the mustard shrub rolled up so that when you place it down it will unroll correctly to look like it is growing? These and many, many other things need to be checked to help the presentation of the lesson go smoothly.

There are as many things for the storyteller to check as there are for the doorperson. The importance is equal. *Both the environment and the materials for the lesson are active participants in this form of teaching.*

One of the first things that a child might need when leaving the circle is a rug. It is a good idea to have a rug box with about four rugs rolled up and standing on end. A "rug" is really a rug sample. If you cannot find them at some dealer, cut a rug into pieces about two feet by four feet and if possible bind the edges. Roll the rugs so the colored and pleasant-feeling side is on the outside and stand them on end in the rug box to be ready for the children.

The rug helps the children focus on their work. They are not for sitting. They are for work, although sometimes sitting and even lying down can be one's work. Some lessons in the Godly Play curriculum such as the parables have their own underlay. Other lessons need a rug, so the materials for the presentation can be placed on it to mark the place for the child's concentration.

Whenever you need a rug for a lesson you can show the children, especially the youngest ones, how to get it out and ready for working. With the young children it is important to show them exactly what you want them to do, since they will mimic your actions. With the older children you can be less explicit.

## Getting a Rug

1. Get up from the circle and go to the rug box and say, "Look. Here is the place you come to get your rug for working." Take out the rug and put your arms around it. As you begin to move toward the circle, say something like, "Don't forget to give your rug a hug! We hug our rugs, because we love our work so much."

2. Walk over to the center of the circle, holding the rug in a vertical position parallel with your body. Set it on its end. One of these rugs standing on its end is about the height of the youngest children. Show them how to turn it over on its side. When it is on its side you can unroll it. You have to crawl on the rug as you push the roll out or the rug will curl up behind where it is being unrolled. When the rug is unrolled in this way it leaves the rough side exposed.

3. Move around to the side and turn it over. Now the colored and softer side is up. You need to come around to the side, because some of the little ones are not much taller than the short side of the rug. They cannot turn it over from end to end.

---

The rugs not only help the children focus on their work. They also help children respect the work of others. "We never step on someone's rug," you might say when the occasion arises.

This is not one of those things that needs to be presented to the group as a lesson for everyone at the same time. Instead, this is demonstrated when the occasion arises such as when a child steps on or steps over another child's rug.

It is easy for adults to step over a rug, or a child, or a child's work, but the teachers need to take care to always go around the rugs of the children. This sets the tone in the room for valuing children and their work. The children become more sensitive to this as part of the community of children. Your job is to help set up the little things for this big discovery to be made.

Rugs also are helpful when someone arrives at church school so tired that he or she cannot really be expected to do anything except sit with glazed eyes or disrupt the class out of frustration. When you find a child like this you might say something like, "Bobby, maybe today is a good day for you to make yourself your work. Go and get a rug. Put it in just the right place. Then get a book or some other work you would like to think about and put your head down."

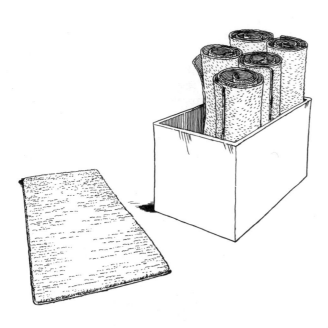

We have had children go sound asleep. Sometimes they are even hard to arouse. If a child has been sleeping and the parents want to know what he or she has done that day, you can always say that the child did very good work. This is absolutely true as it stands, but if the parent presses you for more information it is then that you can say, "Helen needed to be quiet and rest. She did such a good job that she went sound asleep. This was what she needed most this morning."

The church is a safe place. It is a place for Sabbath rest. It is a place where you can come to find peace. It is a place for regrouping. All of this can be taught by the way you organize your classroom and use this method, even for the short time we have on Sunday morning.

## Big Paints

Now let's talk about the "big paints" already mentioned above. They are organized to make them available for children, and they sit on the art shelves next to the watercolors that we call the "little paints." The paints need to be associated with the rugs and the "big white painting trays," so they are stored nearby.

We like to keep the tempera paints in covered containers with a single hole in the center of each top. This keeps the paints from drying out or getting moldy. The single hole in the top guides the child to put a single paintbrush in each color. The paint pots are put in a container that is long enough to have places to set about six paint pots in. This keeps the paint pots from being tipped over. These paint pots and their container can usually be found in school supply stores. The paint pot container is put on the big white painting tray while the children are at work.

The paintbrushes are in a separate basket. We use long-handled brushes with a brush area that is about one-half inch wide. This is part of the reason why this set of response materials is called "big." The "little paints" or watercolors use a smaller container for the colors and the brushes are much smaller.

The big white painting tray also can be found in school supply stores. They are white plastic, so they can be cleaned up easily to look good again. It is hard for children to paint without making a mess, so you want something to control the excess paint that gets spread around and something that really looks fine when they clean it up.

The process for getting ready to paint is big work in itself. The children usually leave the circle with clear intent and much energy. Suddenly, the children, especially the little ones, may slow down as they walk, sometimes even coming to a full stop. This is when the doorperson slips in beside the child, keeping low to help keep the integrity of the community of children intact, and whispers, "Don't you need a rug first?" The doorperson then slips back to his or her chair.

Helping children help themselves takes great skill. It is an art in itself. The child may get out the rug and then get stuck again. "Don't you need a big white painting tray?" The child then goes to get a painting tray and puts it on his or her rug. If the child gets stuck again the doorperson slips in once more and says, "Paint pots and brushes." You can point to where they are on the shelves, and the child begins to move again.

The process continues. The paint pots in their holder are put on the painting tray. The child then remembers the brushes. Off he or she goes again. The child gets the basket with the brushes in it and returns. A brush then gets put in each of the paint pots. This will keep separate the colors, at least in the beginning.

There are other things that the child needs before beginning. The doorperson may need to slip in again and say, "Paper? Big or little?" Then the doorperson points to the shelves where the pieces of paper are kept.

The choice that is proposed to the young child is between two alternatives. This is another way to help the child make decisions. The older children might have three sizes of paper to choose from.

There is still one more thing. What about a painting smock? Spilled paint can become a political problem for the whole church school. People may not care very much about what is taught in church school, but they do care about the clothes their children wear, some of which are expensive. Some painting smocks have sleeves and some do not, use the ones with sleeves if possible.

At first you might think that the problem of spills in the church school is a problem that requires political cover-up as well as the use of smocks. My suggestion is honest and open communication. There will always be spills. They are accidents. No one plans to spill things. What we need most in the church school is mutual understanding with the parents. They need to know what is going on in the church school program, so they can send their children in the kinds of clothes that are appropriate.

Of course, you might want to begin with old, oversized shirts as painting smocks. Invite all of the parents to contribute old shirts. This involves them in part of the solution rather than limiting their participation to only the problem. It also helps communicate what is going on. As with every segment of this approach, you do what you can and what you can afford as your program develops.

The open classroom is a small world in which the way Christian people live together can be shown. We cannot expect children to be able to clean up things like big oil spills when they grow up if they cannot clean up their own small spills in the classroom or at home. We need to show the children how to help maintain the world in a constructive way by providing the tools, showing them how to use them, and giving them the responsibility to care for smaller environments that are appropriate to their age and ability.

*The way that children clean up after their painting is to:*

1. Get the bucket sitting on the supply shelves. Inside the bucket is a placemat to use as an underlay. A plastic placemat is used. Inside the bucket are also a pitcher and a sponge. Beside the bucket on the shelf is a basket filled with clean cloths. Beside it is another basket for the child to put the dirty cloths into.

2. Take the bucket to his or her work area. The place mat is taken out of the bucket and the bucket is placed on it. The pitcher and the sponge are taken out of the bucket and placed on the place mat beside the child's work.

3. Fill the bucket with water. The child takes the pitcher to a water source in the classroom or with supervision goes down the hall to the bathrooms. In either case, a safe way for the child to step up to use the sink needs to be devised, unless the sink is already low enough to use with ease. This is not only for safety, but also allows the child to concentrate fully on filling and emptying the pitcher. The child fills the pitcher to a place marked on the side. Then the child takes the pitcher back to the bucket, and empties the pitcher.

   The child will make several trips back and forth to the water source with the pitcher, until the bucket is filled to a clearly marked place on the side. This may seem like a lot of busy work, but it actually is designed to help ensure that the children, especially the young children, will have success.

4. Dip the sponge into the water and begin to clean up the tray. When the sponge

gets filled with paint it is squeezed into the bucket. More water is absorbed into the sponge and the cleaning continues.

As the child cleans the tray, it gets smeared with the mixed colors. When the paint is thin and almost cleaned up, the child gets one of the dry cleaning cloths to wipe it dry. If the painting tray still is not clean and white again, the process is repeated until the tray shines. The reason for making a special point out of the "big white painting trays" is that they clean up nicely, so they provide a built-in signal for the child. He or she knows when the task is done, because the tray sparkles.

When the child is finished with a cleaning cloth it is put in the basket for the dirty cloths. The doorperson checks this basket at the end of class and takes the dirty cloths home for washing.

It is ideal if the children can do the washing of the dirty cloths and dry them for the next week. This is much easier in a two hour class than in the traditional forty-five minute class on Sunday morning. Nevertheless, the more the children can do to care for their environment, from watering plants to cleaning and repairing materials, the better they can understand that such care is a major part of the way Christian people live together in this world God has given us.

The point is that each child needs to know how to clean up after himself or herself. You can't expect children to do this unless you have organized the room in a way that makes available the tools they need and provided them with a clear process they can understand to do the cleaning. There are other things you can do to get your room organized so the children can care for their environment.

> ### ☞ Helpful Hint:
>
> Whenever there is a spill or something that needs to be cleaned up, the response of the storyteller and the doorperson, whoever is closest, is "That's no problem. Do you know where the things are that are used to clean up?"
>
> The child takes the appropriate basket to the spill. The child sprays the spill and rubs it with the sponge to clean it. If the sponge needs to be squeezed and used again the child can go to the bucket where other children may be cleaning up after their painting work.
>
> There is not a bucket with this type of cleaning. We want the children to have to work out with each other (and the support and help of one of the co-teachers) how to share the tools they need to accomplish their tasks.
>
> When the spill or smudge is wet and loose the drying cloths can be used. The child goes to the clean drying cloth basket and gets one. When he or she is finished it is returned to the basket for the dirty drying cloths. Again, the baskets for the cloths may be in use, so children may need to work out with others their need to use a clean cloth.

Next to the items for cleaning up after painting is a different kind of basket. The distinction in baskets is used to distinguish what is inside and how it is to be used. Inside the basket for general cleaning put a spray bottle and a sponge. The cloths will come from the same baskets as used for cleaning up the big white painting trays.

The plastic spray bottle has water in it, but it is good to use a bottle made from a light-colored plastic. This makes the water more potent-looking and official-looking.

Of course, as at home, a roll of paper towels is a staple item on your supply shelves. This is the quick answer for cleaning up most spills. The problem is that it is too easy and it does not require thinking out how to use the tools provided and sharing them with other children.

The single roll of paper towels might need to be used by several children at once, but this is still too easy. Of course, there are times when the focus is not on cleaning up but on another part of the morning's process. That is when the roll of paper towels is most useful and appropriate.

The children are watching to see if the adults are going to jump, shout, or lose control in some other way when there is a spill. What you are teaching by slowly and carefully cleaning up the spill or having the child do so, if he or she knows how, is that spills happen. The important thing, indeed the natural thing, is to clean them up without a fuss. Every move you make in this teaching environment shows the children what it means to be a Christian person. Taking care of the environment is a large part of this teaching.

## Little Paints

We have already described how to get out the big paints. What about the little paints? You begin with a rug and a big white painting tray, as you did with the big paints. Besides being easy to clean up, this tray is important because sometimes the watercolor paintings, like those made with tempera, become saturated. The plastic tray has sides that help control where the paint goes and its surface keeps the paint off the rug and the floor.

Next, get some paper. For the little ones there is a choice between the big and little paper (nine by twelve inches or eighteen by twenty-four inches). The older children have other alternatives. In fact, they are encouraged to cut the size they need, if they wish. Once a child has a rug, a tray, and the paper it is time to get the paints.

The watercolors are on a shelf near the big paints. Everything that is needed is sitting on a single tray. The box of paints is long and has maybe six or eight colors in little ovals in a row. The plastic box is long enough to have a place in it for the paintbrush. In using these paints, we want the children to use one brush, and to clean it each time before touching another color. That is why the tray that holds and organizes these materials includes a sponge, and a clear container of water with a lid on it.

The child carries the tray over to his or her rug and puts it down. The container of water is the first object that needs attention. It is clear, so the children can see whether the water in it is clean or dirty. When it becomes dirty the child takes it to the water source to pour it out and add clean water.

The child takes off the top of the container to use the water inside. The top is kept on the container until it is sitting beside the child's work. This helps avoid spills as it is carried.

The child then selects a brush. He or she dips it in the water and taps it one, two, three times. He or she then touches it to one of the colors and begins to paint. The first time a child gets out the little paints the doorperson shows this process to the child and actually says slowly, "Tap one, two, three times," while illustrating what to do.

When the child is finished with that color the brush is put in the water and swirled around. Next, it is taken out and tapped on the side one, two, three times, and a new color is selected.

The sponge that is on the tray is for spills, but it has another use too. Sometimes the child senses that there is too much water on the paper. The sponge is then used to soak up some of that excess water from the picture.

You might think that the storyteller ought to present a group lesson to show how to get out work like the little paints. Sometimes that is useful in a brand new class, but the more personal approach is closer to the actual use of the material. Also, this method does not take precious time away from the lessons by the storyteller about the language of the Christian people. In addition, this is another situation where children can help each other to show how Christian people live together.

Most of the time we have found that the doorperson can show this process to each child as he or she leaves the circle. By now you can see that there are many reasons why the children leave the circle one at a time to get out their work. Letting all of the children go at once promotes chaos to be sure, but moving one at a time also helps the co-teachers help the children better help themselves.

## Drawing Boards

Children might want to work on the drawing boards in the room if they are not painting. These are stacked by the painting trays. The children put a board on their rug, and work with colored pencils, felt markers, or other art items that do not involve water. Often, the older children also use drawing boards even when they do use water, but they are better able to control spills at this age.

The colored pencils and the felt-tipped markers are placed standing up in containers. The colors are mixed. Regular pencils are kept in the same way and in the same area of the art shelves. One of the jobs that a child might do to help care for the environment is sharpen all of the regular or the colored pencils. This depends on the age of the child, since we want children to have succees with the things that they do.

Usually the pencils are sharpened as needed. This means that you need a good pencil sharpener in your room. An electronic one gives the most satisfaction and takes up the least amount of the child's time. It has its dangers but they are not as great as the sharp blades in the sharpeners that require the child to twist around by hand. In addition hand pencil sharpeners are hard to use with success for the younger children. When a child needs to sharpen a pencil for the first time, the doorperson illustrates how the pencil sharpener is used.

The markers and the colored pencils are used by getting out a rug and rolling it out in just the right place. The child then goes and gets a painting tray or a drawing board. The drawing boards are various sizes. Some are about three by three feet and have a clip at the top to hold the paper steady. They are made out of some kind of pressed wood, so they can be thin and light. This makes them easy to handle.

When the rug and drawing board are ready. The child gets the desired paper and puts it on the board. He or she then goes to the art shelves and gets a container of pencils or pens. Each container ought to have all of the colors in it. Some will not, of course, but this is one of those things that the doorperson checks before class. If the right color is not in the container the child goes to check the other containers. He or she might need to ask other children also working with the pens or pencils to borrow the color that is needed but missing.

Again, there are not enough pens and pencils for all of the children. You already understand the purpose for this. Children need a real situation in which to work out their ability to share and discuss how to work together. As was the case with the big paints, the doorperson or the storyteller might need to go with a child to help him or her ask for help. This is hard to do, even for adults, but it is important. We do not want to only talk in Sunday school about how Christian people live together. The children need to learn this from what they do in Sunday school.

## Other Media

The art shelves need to contain many media for the children to use. We do not want to prevent the children from making a response because they are not comfortable with the media provided. This means that in addition to the tempera, watercolors, pencils, colored pencils, and markers mentioned above, you will also need clay, scraps of wood, wire, cloth, different kinds of paper, and other things you think the children would like or what they ask for. Each medium is set up in its own container.

At about the age of six to nine, children begin to think about writing things in a journal. Many are not very comfortable with their writing and reading, but some children will be ready for this sort of work. They may choose it if they know the journals are available while other children are working with the tempera, watercolors, clay, wood, or some other medium to express themselves.

For children who would like to write in a journal, show them where you keep the booklets. If you get surprised by such a request just tell the child that you will have one for him or her next time. I like to use those books with the fancy covers and blank pages.

Remember that a journal is private. Even in my research classes I always ask for permission to read the children's journals. Some children have thought over my request carefully and have gone back to glue some of the pages together before they gave their books to me.

Clay is a bit more complicated to make available to the children than the wood, wire, cloth, and other kinds of media. It needs to be kept soft, so it is stored in closed plastic containers. Before class the doorperson checks to see if each container has several small balls of clay in it. When the child opens the container these little balls give them an appropriate amount to begin a project with.

We have two clay containers, one or two baskets of tools, and four or five clay boards for about twenty children. Each clay container might have as many as five or six small balls of clay rolled into a diameter of about two inches.

We use very good clay. It is expensive, but it stays soft until it is baked. Some clay also will stay white when it is baked. This is a good idea, so the children can paint it with good success and sometimes extraordinary beauty.

Sometimes children make things that are too big and in fact waste clay, because they do not realize that they can tear off smaller bits to work with. The small balls of clay help with this and are also easier to warm with their hands by rolling and working them.

The containers for clay are kept on the art shelves beside small boards for clay work. There is also a basket with rolled, clear plastic underlays nearby. Children do their clay work on these so the clay will not stain the surface that it touches. Sometimes they work on the drawing boards laid on a rug or they work at "kneeling tables." These are low tables the children can gather around to work on clay projects and other things in groups by kneeling on the floor.

You will need a few kneeling tables that are big enough to be used for group work, but a few smaller tables are needed as well for single work. It is important to have settings in which either outward-tending or inward-tending children can be comfortable.

In the clay area there are also one or two baskets filled with clay tools. These help the children draw on the clay, cut it, smooth it, and give it shape. Again, there are not enough clay tools to go around, so the children will have to work together to decide when and how to use them.

When children do not become invested in their clay work, you need to visit with them about rolling their snakes or snowmen back into the little balls to be put into the containers until the "next time." "Snakes" are made by merely taking a ball and rolling it between your hands. It sometimes just happens as a child begins to work with clay. A "snowman" is made by sticking the little balls together, one on top of the other, or by combining clay to make the spheres different sizes. Neither needs much intent to fashion. They are the first steps in an exploration of clay as a medium for expression.

Of course, you need to be careful, even about snakes and snowmen. You need to listen to the children to see if these explorations of the medium do have some special meaning for them.

Special meaning can, of course, be helped by using the approach taken with Arthur in chapter 3. For example, if a child makes one snake, you and the child might walk along the shelves where the sacred stories are kept. If nothing seems to connect for the child you might even suggest that he or she needs to make two snakes for the story of Noah's Ark. This might lead to many pairs and even an Ark as this narrative is explored with deep play. Snowmen might link to Creation and when they melt they might need to be rolled into balls and go back into the clay container for next time.

When a child has finished his or her clay creation it is taken home by the doorperson and baked. When it is returned the next week, the child may choose to continue working with the image and paint it. He or she needs to get a rug and usually a drawing board as well. Sometimes the child will go to one of the kneeling tables to paint the object.

The paint used to finish the clay work is kept on the art shelves in tall baskets so the tubes can stand up on end. Next to the basket on its own tray is a water bottle with some smaller pieces of paper about six-by-six inches. A basket of small brushes sits next to the paper. The kind of paint we use is nontoxic and of high quality, so the colors will be vivid.

The child puts down the paper and then squeezes out the colors that will be needed into little lumps on it. He or she then puts the tops back on the tubes. A paintbrush is placed by each little dab of color to help keep from mixing the colors.

Only a little water is used on each brush. The colors need to be used without being thinned, so they will stay lively and bright. When the water is used for cleaning the brushes, they are swirled around in it and then tapped one, two, three times before being used again.

When the child has finished working with his or her clay object it is put on another piece of paper with his or her name on it and saved. The child puts this and other works in progress that need to be saved on a special set of shelves for safekeeping.

The children need to know that in your classroom the teachers do not lose children's work. This helps them over time to begin to invest themselves in their work and to respect what they do as much as you do. The problem for the teacher is that sometimes this is hard to accomplish, but we must try our best to keep the children's unfinished work. These expressions of their feelings need to be taken seriously.

It is not easy to express what one discovers in an encounter with God's Word. It seems there is always more to be learned and understood. The use of the art materials gives the child a way to probe such mysteries. The expressions in art by the older children often need several weeks to explore the language of Christian meaning.

The children do not control the time they come to the class. Sometimes it will be many weeks, even months, before a child returns to your room. When they return they need to find the work in progress waiting for them. If we do not do this we risk a kind of "theological burning."

David Elkind has written about "intellectual burning." Theological burning is even more harmful. In ordinary school, Elkind has observed, children learn not to invest themselves deeply in their work, because of the way the school day is organized. No one really means for this to happen. It is one of those hidden things that is taught.

The school day is organized into periods for each subject. When you are working on math and the time is up, you switch to another subject, social studies for example. Suppose that you are trying to understand why carry-over or borrowing really works. You were able to check your simple adding and subtracting by hiding your fingers under your desk and actually counting things out (even if all you are supposed to do is memorize your combinations), but how do these operations really work with larger numbers? While you are wondering, you suddenly have to stop and switch to social studies.

What concerns me is that when intellectual burning takes place, the "wondering-about-why" gets lost. Timekeeping is not related to the way each child learns or what he or she is learning at the time. It is related only to an abstraction, the average child, and how that child, who does not exist, learns by another abstraction, the clock.

Theological burning is especially important to keep in mind, because existential issues are very personal. They are full of mystery that cannot be analyzed away. What has been written by others for children to memorize may be helpful, but a faith to live and die by is not one that is borrowed or secondhand. It needs to be our own.

I realize that discovery learning does not work for every child. I also realize that at certain points you need to take stock to see if all of the children you are working with have learned the minimum they need to know to move on to the next level. Furthermore, I know that sometimes you need to have a child memorize how to do something, long division for example, rather than understand how the process works.

An example of when a child needs to memorize a procedure rather than understand why it works is when he or she can't keep up with his or her classmates. In this situation the frustration builds up and the creative process shuts down. The child begins to feel incompetent, worthless, and like an outsider. I understand all of this, but there is something different about religious education and discovery learning.

Religious education is about "why." It is about meaning. Religious education is about an encounter with the living God. It is this relationship which gives meaning beyond neat and complete answers to simple and limited questions. It is this relationship with the Creator that can foster the creative power to move forward in one's journey in constructive ways.

Religious education is about things you cannot explain. It is about coping with existential issues, such as your own death or the need for existential meaning to live. What needs to be discovered is not something that can be solved on the surface like math combinations or the procedure for long division, as important and as useful as math is for the job it does best.

If we theologically burn children in church school and teach them not to explore, we are teaching them that their feelings and their expressions of existential meaning do not count. Their theological explorations are not worth keeping. Their creative encounter with their own absolute limits does not need to be carried through to completion. Sometimes we even teach by default that children ought to pretend that they do not have any existential concerns.

When we teach children to love this language, this community-making and meaning-making set of symbols used by Christian people, we have done something profoundly important. If we can teach the children the art of how to use this powerful language to make meaning for their lives we have done even more. What is most important, however, is to teach the children to know that they have inherited this profound way of being together and of making meaning. It was given to the Christian people, because they do count, each one. This is a gift given to them before they were even born!

One of the ways we can teach all of this is by respecting children's work. Not losing it is only part of this climate of respect, but it is a very tangible part. Children's work is the personal meaning they have made about what matters to them about life and death. It is substantial theology.

We have already mentioned many things about cleaning up the environment. We turn now to the place where the tools for general care of the environment are kept. These are the supply shelves.

## The Supply Shelves

The tools the children need for cleaning up and caring for their environment are on the supply shelves. We have talked mostly about the things needed to clean up after making an art response or when there is a spill. There are just a few more things on the supply shelves that need to be mentioned.

Some tools have to do with dusting. A feather duster is an old-fashioned but practical device that can be

hung up at the end of a shelf or on its front. The feather duster is a good choice for children to use, because they can dust the shelves with materials on them and not disturb the materials too much. This provides a kind of built-in control of error. When you bump something with a feather it usually doesn't break, so the price you pay to notice that you need to be more careful is not too high. This is important, because if the price is too high it can block the pleasure of cleaning.

Children also can help clean the floor. Use a brush and dust tray. Get a small one, so the children can coordinate these two tools successfully. This is better than a dust-buster or a small carpet sweeper, because it is more physical. The child gets more involved. The result is more easily seen as a product of his or her labor.

The use of a more advanced, easier, and more efficient technology can sometimes hide the personal aspect of caring for the environment. The lesson becomes one about running a machine rather than cleaning as personal caring.

A third thing that needs to be added to the supply shelves is a set-up for polishing metal. In a Godly Play classroom there are materials made of metal, such as a small cup and plate which the children label, calling the cup a chalice and the plate a paten, and learn their use for worship. Such materials also are used for teaching how the process of caring for such things can become a kind of prayer.

We buy most of our metal things from stores that sell inexpensive brass items. They tarnish well! There is something for the children to polish nearly every Sunday.

On a tray you need to put a little basket with polishing cloths. You might want to use liquid polish and application cloths. I now prefer a kind of cottonlike material already saturated with polish. It comes in a can. For the child (and the adult) this gives quicker gratification for a job well done than using liquid polish while still remaining personal. The application time is short and the polishing time is as long as you want it to be. Children sometimes used to get bogged down in the application of the polish and wear out before they got to make things shine.

After the piece of the cottonlike material is pulled from the larger bundle in the can it is rubbed over the metal plate, cup, candlestick, or other item until it turns a cloudy black. The polishing material is then thrown away. The lid needs to be put back on the can before the whole set-up is put back on the shelf. The child then uses a polishing cloth to make the metal shine. When the polishing cloths become dirty they can be put in one of the baskets for dirty cloths.

# Work Days

It is difficult to get everything done on some Sundays. Sometimes the opportunity for a response gets squeezed out, so every three or four weeks declare a "work day." This is a day when the children come in, make the circle, and do not have a lesson. The storyteller begins at once to go around the circle to ask the children what work they would like to get out. Following the work period you return to the normal pattern of putting things away and getting ready for the feast. The feast will be discussed in the chapter that follows.

The open access classroom gives the children many opportunities to learn, through experience, how Christian people live together. Learning this for yourself requires making a number of choices. The point of the open classroom is to give the children an opportunity for choices among constructive alternatives.

Making choices also is important if we expect the children to make the powerful language they have inherited their own. Choices are a large part of how children learn how they can live and worship together as Christian people in community as responsible individuals.

# Chapter 4

# The Feast

The involvement of the community of children in what we call "the feast" is an indirect preparation for their participation in Holy Communion. The storyteller does not talk to the children about Holy Communion when the feast is being shared unless a child brings it up. Instead, he or she enjoys the feast with them and allows them to discover the many connections on their own.

Holy Communion is of fundamental importance to nearly all Christian people. Regardless of your worship tradition or the curriculum you use in religious education, the primary place to help the children begin to approach this holy mystery is in the place where they will meet the sacrament itself. This is true about Holy Baptism and other rites too, but the focus here is on Holy Communion.

Take the children into the church and invite the people who prepare Holy Communion to show the children the materials that are used and how they are cared for. The children will be able to understand these things better when they are presented in the actual worship setting.

If the children do not learn how to identify, name, and value these things, their participation will not be as focused or as deep. Their awareness will be a blur of names and objects. When the children are not intentionally introduced to Holy Communion, what they think is happening will be left to chance, so misappropriations of meaning are bound to take place.

The children need to have the objects used by your tradition named and identified by the people who care for and love them. There are often very moving stories associated with these symbols and how they came to be given to your church. The children need to know why these objects are so beautiful, regardless of whether they are ornate or simple in design, and how caring for them is a kind of prayer.

Of course, your Sunday school curriculum will have additional lessons about the sacraments. These also help the children learn the vocabulary of the rite and to practice the pattern of the ritual. Something, however, is lost, since these lessons are given outside the setting for sacramental communication. The symbols are not as able to speak for themselves.

Understanding how to participate in Holy Communion is important for children who are allowed to participate, but it is especially important for children who are not allowed to participate until they pass certain conditions. These conditions may be held dear by your tradition, your parish, or particular families and are to be respected.

The children who have to wait to fully participate need to know why they have to wait. They need to know that they still are part of the family even if they can't come to the table. Sometimes there are liturgical acts done, such as a blessing, which can show they belong while they are waiting. This needs to be explained.

A series of family-centered sessions of instruction about the sacraments is a good way to make sure that the children, the family, and the clergy are communicating the same things about the sacraments. These sessions can culminate on the great day of a baptism or the first time a child receives Holy Communion. The occasion might be marked by the family bringing the gifts forward in the liturgy. The occasion also can be announced in the bulletin, so the whole parish can share their joy with them. Family and friends need to be encouraged to celebrate together with a special meal after church in the home or some other place important to the family.

This brief description of situations in which children can learn about the sacrament of Holy Communion shows that the feast is not critical to this learning. What is critical about the feast is that it have the same sense of celebration and thanksgiving as the Eucharist. The exuberance of a sacrament is there but not the vocabulary of one.

We turn now to a description of the feast in the church school setting. We are creatures, made things, so we need to seek out a significant relationship with our Creator to become whole human beings. This sense of questing together in gratitude gives the feast its special and profoundly playful character. We cannot control the mystery, we only participate in it like a child.

# Putting the Work Away

When it is time for the children to put their work away and get ready for the feast, the storyteller goes to the light switch in the room and turns off the light. If your room does not have any outside windows, only turn off most of the lights in the room. This is to get their attention.

Say to the children, "Listen." Wait for a moment. "Listen. Let me see your eyes." Wait until you actually do see all of their eyes. "I need to speak to everyone all at once. It is time to put your work away. You don't need to hurry. You have all the time you need, but it is time to put your work away now." Your voice needs to be paced and inflected to show that there is no panic about this. You continue, "When you have put your work away come to the circle, so we can get ready for the feast."

When the children have begun to put their work away, turn the lights back on. The storyteller then goes and sits down again in his or her place to anchor the circle as the children return to it. This is a time for visiting with the children as the circle builds again.

The doorperson is very busy during this time. He or she helps the children help themselves, and each other, as they get ready for the feast. As has already been mentioned, this takes more care, patience, and competence than putting things away for the children. While continuing to guide the activity in the room, the doorperson also gathers three children to help with the feast.

Sometimes the storyteller will need to leave the circle to help some of the children. This usually occurs with young children. The decision about when to do this is very difficult, because the little ones also need the storyteller to anchor the circle and visit with them. There is no rule for this special problem. It requires balance and experience to know when to do what.

## Preparing for the Feast

While the children are visiting in the circle with the storyteller the doorperson is working with the three children who will serve the feast. The doorperson goes to the door and brings inside a basket with napkins in it. A tray with cookies or something else to eat is also brought in. Finally, the tray with the drinks already poured into little cups is carried into the room.

How did these things get set up outside the room? As you can see, the attention of the storyteller and the doorperson is needed in the room. Getting all this ready outside the room would be at the expense of helping the children help themselves with their work so this is the task of the feast people, which will be described in a moment.

When the children "set the table" they begin with the napkins. Next come the cookies or other things to eat. Finally comes the juice. It is the juice that is most likely to give problems, so we leave it exposed to accidents the least amount of time.

Children are not served unless they are ready. By this I mean that a serving child will not put down the napkin, cookie, or juice unless the waiting child is sitting with his or her legs crossed and hands folded, resting on the ankles. This is not discussed, but the children are reminded. "Remember, you need to be ready to be served."

The feast is prepared by a group of "feast people." They take turns preparing these things. They go to a nearby storeroom where the napkins, juice, and cookies are kept and bring what is needed to the classroom area. They count the children and teachers and prepare the right amount of napkins, juice, and cookies. This is left near the door on a table. When the co-teacher opens the door everything is ready.

Some people in the church family are at a place in their lives where despite their willingness to help, they cannot commit to the schedule of preparation and teaching that a doorperson or storyteller needs to. They could come to many of the teacher's meetings, and that is a good idea, but they cannot commit to teaching every Sunday. Being a feast person gives them a way to help with the time they have.

We have found over the years that signing people up Sunday by Sunday is confusing and too time consuming. It is better to sign up once a year for a whole month than try to keep track of a week by week schedule. In addition, people learn better what to do and feel more a part of the church school when they come for a whole month.

The supply room is where the feast people gather first. It is there that they find the things they need as well as a posted outline of their duties. The carts are kept there for them to use to distribute the things for each room. This may sound a bit strange or perhaps unchristian, but we finally had to chain our carts together so they could be found on Sunday morning. That adds to the fun. The feast people are also the keepers of the carts. They have the keys to unlock them. In addition we put fierce rubber snakes on the carts to startle potential borrowers or at least to remind them of their fallen state.

As a class is drawing to a close the doorperson is supposed to make a count after most of the children have arrived and write it on a gummed note pad and stick it on the outside of the door or on a nearby table. Sometimes this does not get done, because of the com-

> **☞ Helpful Hint:**
>
> When children do not want what is being served, ask them to say, "No thank you." The servers will then pass them by. Normally, no substitute is offered for the things being eaten on a given day. If children do not like what is offered to drink they can choose a cup of water that is included on the feast carts.

**Helpful Hint:**

Suppose that there is a spill when you are sharing the feast. When a child knocks over his or her cup of juice you might say something like, "That's okay. Do you know where the paper towels are?"

The doorperson may need to model a few times how to do this. Go to the shelf where the paper towels are and bring the roll to the spill. Set it down on its side beside the spill with dramatic care. Pull out one square. Stop. Look at it and then slowly tear off the single square. Put the square to one side. Repeat this until you have three or four squares, depending on the size of the spill. Place the one square down. Is that enough? You put down other squares of paper on top of each other. Press down carefully. Pat the paper squares. Fold up the wet squares of paper and carry them slowly and carefully to the wastebasket and put them (not throw or drop them) inside.

plexity of the morning. The feast people notice this and make the count for themselves by looking through a window or stepping into the room for a moment.

On special occasions, such as Christmas and Easter, special breads, napkins, and things to drink are brought by the feast people. Their creativity is important to the whole enterprise. Some people love working out something new for these special times. Others prefer the regular Sundays and preparing their standard fare.

Our research groups, which meet for two hours on Saturday, have a more substantial feast. They have cheese, fruit, and some kind of healthy crackers or bread. The bread often is spread with some kind of all-fruit spread. There is no reason why this cannot be done on Sundays, except for the time it takes to get this ready and the expense.

No child likes every kind of juice and cookie. This is no great revelation. The best health compromise we found for Sunday morning was oatmeal cookies and apple juice. Yet, week after week of oatmeal cookies and apple juice is too much. Some variety is needed. The feast people can really help with this.

I realize that children do get hungry and thirsty during the forty-five minute "hour," but it is not really a long time. The goal of the feast is not biological. It is not to make the ride home easier or the visit to the church during the next hour more easily negotiated. It is the nourishment of the spirit with which we primarily are concerned.

Sometimes children need to bring their own juice and cookies to meet their need for a special diet. Explain this to the community of children in a matter-of-fact way. Occasionally, the child can bring his or her special juice and cookies for everyone to share.

We do not refill the cups or give out new cookies when something happens to them. This is because such activity can turn into the destructive and time-consuming game of "Spill and Fill."

The process by which the feast is done can also be used at times and places other than in the church school classroom. For example, when the whole church school gathers to celebrate Christmas, Easter, All Saints, or Pentecost, or during an opening or closing session for the year, the children can sit in their class groups. Three children from each group go to the table where the refreshments are kept and return to serve their class while the rest of the children sit in their accustomed circle.

The getting-ready position also moves into general use after a few years. An example of this is when the children are invited to come forward to watch some part of the liturgy, such as a baptism, they will come up and sit down naturally with their legs crossed.

Children like to know what to do. They like to feel competent. They want to participate in an appropriate way. We cannot expect children to be ready to participate unless they know how. This is a skill to be learned, and much of what goes on in a classroom like the one I am describing gives children the bits of behavior they need to serve them well in other settings.

# Sharing the Feast

During the feast preparations the storyteller needs to keep supporting the children. This preparation can take a long time for some twenty children, especially if there is a spill or two.

The storyteller winks, smiles, and says things like: "That's the way. You can do it. This is a long time to wait, but you are doing well. Remember to wait. It's no fun to have our feast until everyone is served. A feast is something we do all together."

When the occasion arises you might say things like: "A feast is not about how much you eat. Some people think that, but they do not understand. It is not even about what you eat. It is about how you share what you have. It is about being together."

A child may say, "This is no feast! It's only juice and cookies." Another child might say "This is not a feast, it's only a snack."

These are the teachable moments. "Oh no, a feast is how you feel about what you share. It is not what you have. Sometimes a feast might be only a little water and a piece of bread. If that is all there is to share then that is a feast. This is why it is so important to wait until everyone is served and to say our prayers."

You also might say, "Did you know that the Jewish people have a feast at about the same time that we celebrate Christmas? The Jewish feast is not about Christmas, but it is about lights in the dark. The feast is called Hanukkah. It lasts for eight days and remembers the time when the Jews could use their Temple again after the Syrians were driven out of Jerusalem and back to their own country."

With an introduction like the one outlined above, you might tell this story for the older children.

———————

*"There was once a little girl who lived in Holland. Her name was Anne Frank. When the Germans marched into her country during the Second World War the Jews had to hide. They were afraid, because the Germans were sending all the Jewish people to camps where they were killed.*

*Anne's family was Jewish, so they crept into a secret place high up under the roof in a big house and began to live there in secret. Another Jewish family joined them in their hiding place.*

*"When it came time for Hanukkah, Anne remembered all the other Hanukkah her family had shared. There had always been lots of food and presents. The secret Hanukkah in the attic was the best one of all, she wrote in her little book.*

*"Anne wrote a lot in her little book. She wrote what happened. She wrote about the birds flying free in the sky as she looked out of the little window. She wrote down the feelings she felt.*

*"A little book in which you write what you think and how you feel is called a journal or a diary. You can still read Anne's journal today. It has been made into a book and even a movie. Her story is called* The Diary of Anne Frank *and you can buy it in stores.*

*"The reason she liked the family's secret feast best of all was because they were all still alive and together. When they had their little bits of food and gave tiny presents it was like saying, 'Thank you,' for just being there together.*

*"I am sorry to say that the Germans did find Anne and her family. They sent her to one of their death camps and she did die. She knew so very, very much about life and death. Children know a lot about such things, you know. Sometime you might want to write down some of the things you know. There are books with blank pages in them in your classroom that you can use if you want to. You too can keep a diary like Anne did."*

———————

*Being ready* is part of the feast, as it is with everything else that is done in the classroom. Only those children sitting cross-legged with their hands on their ankles get their napkins, cookies, and juice. The others are passed by until they are also ready. The servers go around and around the circle until everyone is served. When that is done it is time for our prayers.

Look around the circle. Become aware of your own pleasure at being present in this community of children. Think not only of that moment, but also of the future of this community. Remember your own childhood. Let your feelings catch up with you. It has been a busy morning. Pause as you do this, so your next comments will be filled with these important reflections.

"Just being here is wonderful. Thank you for coming to the circle. Sometimes being here makes us so happy that we just have to say our prayers."

Look around the circle and wait until the children are focused and then say, "There are all kinds of prayers. Some are long and some are short. Some are out loud and some are so quiet that only God hears them. Some prayers are words you remember, words that somebody told you. There are also prayers that are made up from your own words, like talking with a friend. Some are talking prayers, and others are singing prayers. There are all kinds of prayers. I wonder what kind of prayer you will feel like making today? Maybe you won't feel like making one. That's okay. Maybe you will."

"Remember, if your prayer is one of the prayers that is quiet, be sure you say the 'Amen' out loud. We need to know when to go on to the next person."

Then move around the circle with your eyes. Beginning on your right, look at each child and say with your eyes or maybe with a word, "Yes?" The child shakes his or her head up and down or side to side. There is no pressure to pray. If the child signals "No," just move on. Go around the circle. "Yes." "No." "Yes." "No." Sometimes a child will change his or her mind, so you go back.

At the end I like to pray this simple prayer: "Thank you God for these wonderful children and for our feast. Amen."

Sometimes the children laugh a laugh of recognition when they hear my prayer. "Mr. Berryman, why do you pray the same prayer every time?"

"It is because it is true. That is the most important thing about a prayer. It needs to be true. It needs to be the most true of all your feelings and your thoughts. You can tell God anything, but it needs to be as true as you can make it."

Here is another one of those teachable moments. When a child asks an honest question, it means that the mind is engaged and open. Teachable moments are both hard to plan and evaluate, but meeting a child in such a moment makes all the difference.

When the prayers are finished we have our feast. You might say, "Now we can have our feast all together." While the juice and cookies are being shared you visit about school, pets, vacations, family holidays, and the other things that come up. You can't plan this in advance, but you need to have in mind some situations to talk about that you know interest children and will keep them in touch with what is important in life.

This is also a time when the storyteller can tell seasonal stories that are related to the Christian year and life. Tell stories of the saints, of Christmas, of Easter, and of other times and people you have known. Tell stories about your own church family.

The children need to know the stories of the people of their parish, and they need to have those stories mixed in with the stories and legends of other times and places that the Christian people have known. This shows them that the Communion of Saints and life's mystery is still all about us. There is always more to life than meets the eye. There is always more, even in the familiar.

# Putting Everything Away

When the children are finishing the feast the storyteller notices when the first child is ready and says something like this: "Watch how we put our things away. Fold up all your crumbs in your napkin and put your napkin in your cup. Then put your cup in the wastebasket. It is over there." You then act this out with seriousness but with a twinkle in your eye.

The children go one by one to the wastebasket with their things and then return to the circle. The wastebasket is somewhere near the doorperson's seat so he or she can help with this process. No slam dunks are allowed.

All of these operations are difficult for the little ones to do, so they need the support of both the storyteller to guide them and the doorperson to help them accomplish the task with success. The older children need the storyteller to show that putting things away is important and they need the doorperson to be sure they do not get distracted.

You may have already begun to wonder about putting a napkin into a cup that is still filled with liquid. Some children decide they do not want to drink all of their juice. If the napkin is stuffed into the cup the juice might overflow.

Part of what I mean by "support" is to watch for these problems and anticipate them if possible. The storyteller might say something like: "Remember, if your cup is too full you can take your napkin in one hand and the cup in the other hand. Put them both carefully into the wastebasket."

You often need to tailor your support to each child. When you notice that a cup is about half full you could say: "Remember that if your cup is about half full you can still put your napkin in your cup. Put it in carefully. Don't let the juice run over the sides of your cup as you put the napkin inside."

As children are walking toward the wastebasket, you need to remind them that the wastebasket has a plastic liner, so they can put juice into it without it leaking out the bottom onto the floor. This helps at home and in other places where there may not be a liner and a liquid might seep out.

"Remember, the wastebasket has a plastic liner inside. This will catch your juice, so it will not run out and get on the floor. Always check to see if a wastebasket will hold what you pour inside before you pour it in. Sometimes you need to put your juice in the sink or ask someone to help you." Obviously, this bit of language is directed toward the younger children, but it is surprising how such things need to be repeated over and over again each year for the children to really hear them and to make that bit of action their own.

I enjoy repeating things to the older children that I know have been said to the younger ones, but I do this with a sense of humor. The implication is that we both know that older children know this, but I'm saying it again because I'm being a little silly, playing with them.

By the time the children in the circle have begun putting their feast things away and are returning to the circle, there are parents waiting at the door to pick up their children.

The next step in the Godly Play process is saying good-bye. This will be described in the next chapter.

# Chapter 5

## Leaving

This chapter completes the flow of the Godly Play process, by describing how to help the children say good-bye and cross the threshold back into the world of the everyday.

I am not suggesting that the function of the church or church school is limited to being a retreat from the world for reflection and renewal. The Christian people are a people of both being and doing. This is why the integration of spiritual reflection with ethical action in the community of children has been one of the main themes throughout this book. Being and doing cannot be separated without the disintegration of the whole person.

When a child steps into this place the trance of the everyday world can be broken. One of this method's goals is to make evident the "anti-structure" to ordinary reality so the child has a chance to experience why the structures of everyday life do not fully satisfy us. This is as important for adults to experience as it is for children.

The structures and the language of everyday experience tend to insulate us from the power of the encounter with the presence of the mystery of God. Many church school programs and churches get taken over by everyday concerns and ordinary views of reality. Where this happens the threshold of the church or the church school makes no difference. No anti-structure is provided inside the place by which to challenge what is thought to be "normal." No different language is taught or used to discover the alternative reality Jesus called the kingdom of heaven.

I fully understand why many churches and church schools prefer not to acknowledge the theological challenge to the language and reality of everyday living in their programs. A place that is set apart for Christian people to discover who they truly are is not all superficial fellowship and feeling good. Instead, such a place acknowledges ambiguity, the wildness of the imagination and the power of the Creator. No attempt is made to try to keep God in a cute little box.

Pilgrims who enter such places need to be guarded by symbols and supported by rituals to keep from being overwhelmed. We need good and wise companions to learn how to make this journey and to return with new direction and meaning.

Church and the church school are places to learn that we are not God. The identity of the human creature cannot be known without such a discovery. If we do not know our limits, how can we know who we are? Death is part of life. We are fearfully free. Aloneness needs to be appreciated to understand community. We can't live fully without ultimate meaning.

Many people like to pretend that children—early, middle, and late childhood people—do not sense the existential issues in life. Adults pretend that children do not bump up against such absolute boundaries. Such a defensive pretense sometimes even gets taught as the religion of the Christian people. The Godly Play process of learning how to speak and be Christian stands in complete contrast to such a hidden curriculum.

It is a profound step for the children to take when they enter and leave an environment where existential issues are acknowledged, ultimate boundaries accepted, and where the presence of the mystery of God is eagerly expected, yet awaited with awe.

# Acknowledging the Parents

The parents begin to gather outside the door toward the end of the education hour. The door person needs to remember that they come to that door with many needs, as they did when they brought their children.

Some parents wonder about their children. Did they do well? Others are in a hurry to get to their next destination. Some would like to visit, but at this moment you do not have time. They all want what they want, so the doorperson must act with care to continue to help protect the community of children and the sense of this environment as a special place while managing the transition at the doorway in a constructive way.

Of course, educating the parents can help them know how to come to the door and what to expect. Still, many will not make time for such education, and others will not understand something so different from their own *school* experience. Other parents will be new to the church, and may not have heard what we are doing. Most parents come to the door with anxiety, not knowing what they are on edge about.

The doorperson opens the door at the end of the hour to see who is there. Some parents may have already tried to get their child or children early. Choose a time that is not charged with the emotions of the doorway to try to explain, in detail, how the transition is made. The doorperson might say something like: "I'll call this week, so we can talk. I know this is a bit different. Don't worry about it. We'll talk. I look forward to it."

Sometimes parents will try to come into the room without respecting the threshold. There are good reasons for this. They want to take part in and support their child's experience. Others need to show themselves and their children that they are really in charge, even if you are the church school teacher. That is okay. Some parents must do such things. Help them gradually to trust the process. It makes sense. There is a logic to it which can be stated. Ask them to be teachers or feast people so they can get acquainted with what is going on and get to know the people who have accepted the responsibility for this kind of leadership.

> **Helpful Hint:**
>
> In one church where I worked, we looked for the most respected person we could find to stand outside the doorway to interpret what was going on inside the classroom. This took some of the pressure off of the doorperson.

Parents feel good if they can talk with someone recognized as a leader in the church, and such a person lends his or her credibility to this part of church life. The church school and the people who work there are sometimes discounted, because they are not involved in so-called "adult" concerns. When the parents learn that they have deeply happy children in a program like this, they will relax. Some will even realize that there is no more important adult concern than the nourishing of children to become truly human.

There are many things that make a child profoundly happy in this process. Fundamentally, the joy comes from having a basic need met. This need is to acknowledge the existential limits to one's life and to learn a language that can help cope with life's ultimate mystery.

It is our relationship with God which gives the greatest meaning to life. This relationship is part of a whole system of relationships that include the child's relationship with his or her deeper self, with others, and with nature. When any one of these relationships is carefully and respectfully honored, all of the relationships benefit. The name of each child is a very important symbol of your relationship with him or her.

# The Child's Name

Of course, we need to know the children in our classrooms. We need to send them notes in the mail. Children love to get mail. We need to remember the day of their baptism. We need to do all sorts of things to make our connection with them and with their families and church family lively and real. It is the name that symbolizes all of this, and the way you say that name that tells the child how you value the relationship.

I don't always remember children's names. I am not good at that, but I do remember everything about them and their families. That comes easily, and helps with the relationship, but it is the name, symbolizing our relationship and all that I know about the person, that escapes me. Often, the first name is there, but I have to work to have the whole name come easily to mind. It takes time and effort for some of us to be fluent with people's names.

The Good Shepherd called the sheep by name. I am clearly an ordinary shepherd, but I share the values of the Good Shepherd, and I want to make them my own to the best of my ability. I fail, and I try again.

Names are an important part of saying good-bye. At the end of the class the doorperson opens the door a bit to see who is there. As parents arrive the doorperson whispers into the room the name of the child the parent is there to pick up.

In the circle the storyteller continues supporting the children who have their legs crossed and their hands folded on their ankles. As in other cases, the child needs to be ready to participate. Only the names of the children who are ready are called.

If a child is not ready, the doorperson passes that child by and whispers the name of another child whose parent is there. If a parent notices his or her child being passed over, the doorperson might say, "I'm sorry, Mary isn't quite ready. While she's getting ready I'll call Bobby's name and then I'll come back to her."

The parents need to have their waiting framed in a positive way. As you remember, one of the primary goals of this method is to have every child leave the room with a positive experience. You don't want the parents to come down on a child the minute he or she steps out of the room because they made the parent wait.

When the doorperson calls a child's name the child gets up and goes to the storyteller to say good-bye. He or she then crosses the circle to where the door person is seated, moves past the doorperson, and crosses the threshold.

# The Good-bye

The method of saying good-bye described here may seem too formal or old-fashioned, but there are many reasons for using it. Remember that the storyteller is sitting on the floor. This enables the child to walk up and look the adult in the eye. The difference in size is neutralized by the standing child and sitting adult. The older children can even look down on the storyteller.

The storyteller holds out his or her hands as the child approaches. Some children will shake hands. Others will take hold of both the offered hands. Sometimes, especially the little ones, give the storyteller a hug. Some will continue to stand there in front of the storyteller. What is important is that the child has options.

All the adult can do is make the invitation with open hands. The children do not have to accept it. I respect their feelings about personal space, touching, and how they want to say good-bye. This is not a superficial thing I am asking them to do.

Whatever happens with the hands, I say something like: "You did good work today," and comment on some aspect of what they did. "The painting you made was full of color and life." I like to allow the work to stand on its own merit. It was "good" work, because the child did it, not because I think it was good or bad.

When a child has not made an art response but worked with a material, perhaps with another child, you might say, "I saw you working with Noah's Ark." I leave the sentence open-ended. This is to allow the child to finish the thought. This will give the teacher a clue about where to go next with the supportive conversation. Whether or not the child continues the conversation, you can conclude with, "You were really working well."

Sometimes children will have wandered the whole time. What do you say then? First, you need to decide whether the wandering was constructive or destructive wandering.

Constructive wandering is moving about the room while watching other children work and looking at the things on the shelves. Sometimes this leads to work the child will get out. It might be a warm-up period, but other times it may be the way the child learns. Some children are long-distance learners. You might try to redirect this way of learning toward a closer involvement in a material or art response, but that is not always successful or appropriate. The point is that such wandering is good work in itself.

Destructive wandering is more aimless. The child is afraid to get engaged. When this is sensed by the teachers, the wandering needs to be directed. The teacher's support is needed by the child so he or she can make a decision. Over time this support will enable the child to move with intent.

Constructive wandering is moving with the intent to explore the room and enjoy what the other children are doing. Destructive wandering often results in the child looking for ways to disrupt the work of others. He or she cannot yet engage in an activity, so the child does not like to see the other children busy and focused.

Sometimes you even need to say to an aimless child, "You may not disturb the other children. They are working. Now, what work would you like to get out?" You then repeat the process that is used for helping the children make decisions in the circle, as described in chapter 3.

The child knows whether his or her wandering was learning or evading learning. An aimless child does do good work, nevertheless. The participation in the community of children has challenged the child to learn how Christian people live together.

When the storyteller says good-bye to a child it is almost like a blessing. The relationship only lacks the formal words. This acknowledges the passing of the peace. Remember the term "good-bye" is a contraction of the English expression "God be with you."

Saying good-bye to the child is quiet, focused and intimate. Your voice is soft, so only the child can hear. This is a moment of closeness to make the closure personal and warm.

One must guard against making this intrusive. It is not forced intimacy. All that it intends to show is that you care for, respect, and support the child. It also shows that at another time, even outside of class, the child can approach you with something personal. You have shown him or her that you are at ease with intimacy and closeness. In a crisis of loss or in a time of intense wonder children will know they can trust you because you will be steady in your support. Nothing will shock you or in some other way break the relationship they have found to be trustworthy.

Sometimes a child will get excited with all of this closeness and start to bolt across the room and run out the door. That is why the storyteller reminds each child to walk as he or she leaves the good-bye. "Remember to walk carefully."

At other times a child might be so excited about hearing his or her name called that a direct line toward the door is taken. The doorperson merely redirects the child by saying, "Don't forget to tell Mr. Berryman good-bye." That is usually enough to send the child back for the storyteller's good-bye.

# Going Through the Threshold

As the child goes through the doorway he or she often says good-bye to the doorperson. This is not as formal as the good-bye with the storyteller. It might be a wave. Sometimes the child moves right on past the doorperson and out the door. We let that happen. The primary good-bye has taken place in the circle.

To miss a child's good-bye is sometimes hard on the doorperson, but that is something to be talked about between the co-teachers. Children bless us by their comings and goings, but what is important for the child is that he or she has a personal, clear, and supportive closure. Saying good-bye twice is not essential.

All of this is not to say that the doorperson ignores the child or would refuse a hug, a handshake, or a wave. It is just to say that the good-bye with the doorperson is different from that of the storyteller. Besides, during this time the doorperson also is trying to connect with the waiting adults.

The door person wants to be sure that every adult knows that his or her child has had a good day. This is not "public relations" for the program. It is the truth. The process is set up for such a result, and this is a very natural outcome.

Some children bring nothing but bad reports home to their parents about school. Parents who are used to hearing unhappy things about their children especially need to know that in this place their children have a good day, and each one is considered a uniquely important person. Such reports can change a parent's perception of his

86

or her child and this helps change the child's sense of who he or she really is.

This sort of classroom is a place for affirmation as well as discovery, but the process and the feelings are connected. The creative process does not work well in places where children are under threat of failure or in danger of ridicule. The children need to be able to rely on an environment that is supportive of them.

Sometimes the doorperson needs to redirect a parent's testing at the door. A parent might ask, "What did you learn in Sunday school today?"

Silence.

"What was the lesson about?"

"The Good Shepherd."

"What is the Good Shepherd?"

"A Terrible."

"A what?" Laughter. "Oh, you mean a parable."

Suddenly, the doorperson is alert to this conversation and is listening for an opening to make an intervention.

The "testing" goes on: "Can you tell me the parable of the Good Shepherd?"

All of this is well-intentioned. There is nothing actually said that is very destructive. Whether this sounds constructive or destructive to the child depends on the tone of voice and other contextual clues.

Part of the problem is that sometimes we adults ask children to do things that they are not yet able to do. Retelling a whole story from beginning through the middle to the end is not something that young children are likely to be able to do. They cannot hold a whole narrative structure in their minds as adults can. This is why children often want to hear a story over and over again. It is also why they may tell you an episode in the story, the part that stimulates them most, when you ask them to recall the whole narrative. They are not being evasive. It is one of their developmental limitations.

One of the things that is helpful about using concrete materials in a classroom is that it enables the younger children to keep the whole story in front of them. For example, the parable of The Good Shepherd comes in a gold box. You take the "pieces" of the parable from the box and lay them out on a felt underlay as the story is told. These parts of the parable are laminated figures that slide across the underlay during the telling. Other objects such as water, rocks, and a sheepfold are made of felt like the underlay. It is all there to see and touch, as well as to hear.

With all of this in mind a doorperson might invite the parents of a young child to wait and come back into the room after class. This gives the child a chance to *show* the parent the parable rather than to try to

 **Helpful Hint:**

A parents' night also is a time when the children can present their favorite materials to their parents. These meetings are more like parties than a time to make judgments about "schooling." It is the context of schooling that brings out the judgmental and scolding edge in some adults, because that is the way they were treated as children.

**Helpful Hint:**

There is no reason to try to avoid challenges to this or any program or to teachers. This approach has been used in this way by many volunteers during the last twenty-five years, but there is always more to learn. Questions about teachers and teaching are almost always helpful even when they are not intended to be.

Challenges need to be met with clarity and directness. The people who are doing the complaining, those complained about, and those who make decisions about paid and volunteer personnel need to all sit down in the same room at the same time. All points of view need to be treated with respect and care, because there is much to be learned about ourselves and the art of teaching.

tell it. Even older children (and adults) find the physical markers for the presentation helpful to keep the narrative in place.

It is important for adults to appreciate how important it is for a young child to begin to know the powerful language of the Christian people with his or her body. Such knowledge is different from that of the mind and can inform one's intuition and spirit more profoundly than merely being able to recall a sequence mentally. Inviting the parent or parents to sit down with the child also gives a better setting in which the child can show his or her feelings for the parable rather than merely being tested on the recall of words and a structure.

If the parent chooses not to take the time to slow down and participate in this process, that is fine too. The doorperson has at least interrupted the interrogation. It is time for them to move on to other things.

Another approach is to enter the conversation between the parent and the child with humor. "Oh my, children often call the parables 'terribles.' I think they are right in a way. Parables are hard to understand and sometimes when we finally find the meaning for our lives it is something we are not sure we want to know. Parables can be very terrible!"

In addition to a few remarks at the doorway, the doorperson or storyteller might call during the week to see if the parents would like to come in alone or with their child for a presentation. This is also a good time to tell the adults about a parents' night or a model class. These are occasions when parents can be introduced to the room, the process, and the way the children express themselves in art media and the materials. See chapter 1 for more information.

There are many reasons for the doorperson to be alert as the child passes through the threshold. Sometimes the parents tend to blame the teachers for the child not "knowing" the lesson. Others may blame the program in general for not being successful. Blame seems to be a global response for some people. When this happens, the doorperson needs to keep the focus of the discussion on a specific lesson or Sunday and not allow the blame to become generalized. This takes patience and a strong nondefensive attitude.

Misunderstandings are bound to happen with any curriculum or way of managing a classroom full of children. The bottom line is to be alert to the continuing possibility of

## Troubleshooting

It is a good idea to develop a procedure, and communicate it to the parents, about picking up their children. The child will stay in the classroom in the circle with the storyteller, but this cannot continue indefinitely.

Teachers have things to do after Sunday school as well as parents, so the children cannot remain in the classroom for very long. The teachers may plan to work on their classroom, discuss the morning, or leave.

Here is a suggestion. After about five minutes take the children who are left to the babysitting area. This needs to apply to older children as well as younger ones. Leave a note on the door to indicate the location of the children. This procedure needs to be communicated to parents several times during the church school year.

Part of my caution about this comes from having been a headmaster of a school some years ago. Keeping track of children at fire drills, during the day, and at their arrival and departure is woven into my nervous system. Also, I worked at Christ Church Cathedral in downtown Houston from 1984–1994, where we had a large and growing number of children in a setting that was full of risks for them.

My experience in smaller, more suburban, and even rural churches suggests that care needs to be taken everywhere. The dangers for children range from misunderstandings, which distress both the children and the parents, to divorced or estranged parents fighting over children and taking them without permission. There is always the danger of outright kidnapping or abuse by strangers. Parents may grumble at such care, but when they stop and think about it, they will appreciate it.

misunderstanding and try to remain open to the remarks made by parents. You do not need to defend the teachers or the program when no assault is intended.

When something has gone wrong, be the first to admit it. Let the parents know that what happened is not the goal. You didn't do the kind of job you wanted to.

There are some safety issues about dismissals that must be mentioned now. Only release the children to their parents, unless some other procedure has been previously worked out. You might even want to have exceptions to this policy in writing. A small child's older brother or sister may pick him or her up, for example.

The bottom line is that the children need to find a safe place for their own journey in order to flourish. No matter what your program provides, it may not be a good place for a child if the parents are chronically unhappy with the program. The parents may need to move to another church where they are more comfortable, so the child will be able to relax, feel at home, and begin learning again.

The theme of continuously learning more about ourselves and the art of teaching continues in the next chapter.

# Chapter 6

# Contemplating and Evaluating

When the children leave the room it seems empty, and yet if we pause for a moment we can recall their presence as if they were still there. The community is gone, but the presence of God in that community may remain. To learn from our experience with children, we adults need to take the time to pause and reflect on both the presence of the children and of God in what has happened.

There are two kinds of learning we need to do if we are going to understand what has happened. One we will call *evaluation*. This kind of learning-about-learning, which is usually associated with traditional educational methods, claims objectivity and uses the scientific method. The other kind of learning-about-learning is called *contemplation*, and is subjective, a kind of reflection or recollection, that attempts to take in the whole experience in an undifferentiated way. The spirit of the whole experience is intuited.

If one jumps too soon to objective evaluation, the sense of presence, both of the children and of God, can be missed. It is better to begin with the contemplation of what happened, holding the whole experience in memory, in the quietness of the room after the children are gone.

William Wordsworth (1770–1850), the English poet, loved to use the word *tranquility* to signify the attitude one needs to adopt to recover an almost forgotten sense of presence. Usually, as Wordsworth observed in one of his poems, "The world is too much with us," for this recovery to take place.

Jesus' disciples missed the meaning of the phrase "The Kingdom" for the same reason. They focused on their adult concerns. "Who will be the most important?" they wondered. "How will it be governed?" Jesus answered with a parable of action. He placed a child in their midst. "Unless you become like a child, you will never enter the kingdom of heaven."

This should not be dismissed as a sweet story about children. It is about adults and it is deadly serious. In Matthew (18:6) and Mark (9:42, RSV) it is reported that Jesus also said, "Whoever causes one of these little ones who believe in me to sin, it would be better for him if a great millstone were hung round his neck and he were thrown into the sea." Adults are at risk in religious education as well as children. The learning question has two sides. Will the children learn from the adults? Will the adults learn from the children?

The difference between children and adults is that children can know God unconsciously without even trying. They can be in the Kingdom as part of their assumed world. We adults have a more difficult time, because this presence is neither assumed nor accepted. The world is too much with us. We have unlearned what many of us knew as children.

To regain our own experience of God's presence again we need to consciously try to do it. Yet, as so many have discovered, trying harder can drive God's presence away. We need to take an indirect approach. To stimulate our own awareness of God's presence we need to be aware of what the children around us experience of God, even if they do not have the words to express this yet.

Whether we count and measure or meditate on the presence of God after class, things need to be put away. Some of you will be putting things away to prepare the room for a different use during the week. Others will be preparing the room for next Sunday. Regardless of what you are preparing for it is important to take time during that preparation to begin your learning about what happened.

When you begin with your general and more personal sense of what happened, your intuition can process many more impressions than you can deal with during a conscious analysis. This open or contemplative approach is a way to connect with the spirit of what happened, and it is there in that wholeness that God can be found. Dividing up what happened into bits and pieces for analysis will also yield important discoveries, but that needs to come later after this ruminating about the whole experience.

The better you are able to sense God's presence in the room, the better *religious* educator you will become. The unspoken lesson of the children's spirituality reflecting back to them from you, and your spirituality reflecting back to you from them will speak the loudest. This is the awareness of being rather than doing. It is the passing of the peace that passes all understanding.

# Contemplating the Presence of God in the Classroom

One of the tragic things about the quest for spirituality today is that many people attempt to use a cafeteria approach. Putting a little of this and that on their tray as they pass down the spirituality line does not provide them with the coherence needed physically, mentally, or spiritually to find rest for their restlessness. They need to go more deeply into a single tradition, like that of the Christian people, to find the kind of community and the depth of spirituality that can satisfy their craving.

Adults as well as children need good companions and wise guides for this journey. *The Classics of Western Spirituality: A Library of the Great Spiritual Masters* is a series published by Paulist Press that makes the writings of some of these great guides accessible to everyone. The introductions to these book help the reader approach these companions through their own words. People who work with children need to know more about the spirituality of such people to be able to be more open to what the children have to show us, so we in turn can support them.

Two key books in the series which fit our purpose here are *Richard of St. Victor* and *Bonaventura.* Each book contains several of the most important writings by the master whose name it bears. Richard of St. Victor's definition of contemplation is the definition we will use. Bonaventura's great summation of spirituality in the thirteenth century, much like St. Thomas's summation of philosophy and theology during the same period, will give us the background to continue with a sense of the great tradition that is being drawn on to make the few remarks that follow.

Induction (knowing by the senses) and deduction (knowing by reason) were both considered to be powerful and authentic ways of knowing for Christian people by Richard (d. 1173) and by Bonaventura (1217–1274). Their concern was to present an integrated view of how spiritual knowing by contemplation fit into the integration of all three kinds of knowing necessary for human health.

Richard's famous definition of contemplation was: "Contemplation is the free, more penetrating gaze of a mind, suspended with wonder concerning manifestations of wisdom." This attitude of mind, a state of beholding, was commented on in most of Richard's works. The definition quoted above may be found in his *The Mystical Ark* (1:4).

Bonaventura's description of spiritual development in *The Soul's Journey into God* integrates his three major sources. He joined into a unified picture of human knowing the contemplation of God in nature through the senses, through the mind using reason, and through the direct perception of God's presence through the spirit to give wholeness to the human being.

Bonaventura drew on his own Franciscan tradition to express the contemplation of God in nature. Francis died in 1226 when Bonaventura was still a boy. Bonaventura went on to become a professor at the University of Paris, minister general of the Franciscan Order, a cardinal, and an adviser to popes.

His view of the contemplation of God in the process of the mind was deeply influenced by the writings of St. Augustine, the Bishop of Hippo in North Africa, who died in 430. In Augustine's book *The Trinity*, which his letters show he worked on most of his adult life, he explored the mind, using many analogies, to find God as Trinity. It is not possible to find God there directly, but in the mind remembering itself, understanding itself, and loving itself one can find a way in part to remember, understand, and love the Trinity by whom and in whose image the mind was made and can become wise.

Bonaventura's interpretation of the direct relationship with God depends on the work of an unknown author called the "Pseudo-Dionysius." The name refers to Dionysius the Areopagite who in Acts (17:34) was recorded as hearing Paul preach in Athens, but the mysterious and influential figure we are discussing probably wrote in the fifth or sixth century.

The influence of Dionysius was great on Augustine, Thomas Aquinas, Duns Scotus, Bonaventura, Boethius, and many other later theologians. He traced the limits of language for the spiritual journey. Even biblical language and liturgical symbols can carry us only a portion of the way in our quest, for God is beyond all knowledge that is limited to the senses and the mind. God is no thing and can only be named so as to be addressed, not conceptualized.

At first, Richard of St. Victor and Bonaventura may seem to be too obscure to be good guides for the spiritual journey today. The emphasis of our time has been on the masterly use of science to explore the material and mental worlds. Richard and Bonaventura seem alien to what we are used to in both secular and religious education.

The emphasis of these people, who knew the science of their age, was to distinguish and practice the method of spiritual knowing as well as knowing by the senses and the mind. Since the distinctions between our body-knowing, mind-knowing, and our spirit-knowing were clear to them, the integration of these differences could be a more adequate one than we are likely to make today.

There is one more thing to mention in terms of background to the first kind of learning we can employ to understand our work with the children. It must be remembered that these writers thought and wrote in earlier times and in other languages. Certain key terms they used need some explanation for us to use them in an appropriate way. For example, I have used *reflection* and *contemplation* in an overlapping way.

The Latin term Bonaventura used for contemplating is *speculatio*. The noun *speculum* means "mirror." Writers in general in those days, Bonaventura in particular, thought in terms of what we might call reflection, speculation, contemplation, and consideration when the Latin word *speculatio* was used. The image of a mirror gives us a clue to help discover what this kind of knowing is about.

Contemplation is not sensorial knowing only. It employs the senses, of course, but that is not where the focus is. Receiving data through the senses monitors and records the natural world about us. If we limit our understanding of the children on Sunday morning to this kind of knowing we will miss some of the most important parts of the experience. Minute by minute details can be listed but their significance or meaning is not grasped. That requires the use of the mind and the spirit.

Contemplation is not knowing only by the senses, nor is it the knowing only by the mind. If we limit our knowing to the senses and to the meaning that the mind makes from sensorial awareness we will miss the spiritual dimension of what happens with the children. Evaluation uses the mind, making distinctions and generating theories to be tested by the sensorial facts, but contemplation is more global in its perception. It notices something different.

Now, let's look at these differences by means of some examples. An example of a sensorial description is to write: "Bobby goes to the shelf and gets out the the Parable of the Good Shepherd, which he had just seen presented as a group lesson. He smooths out the underlay slowly and completely. The figures of the parable are moved across the underlay carefully. The words he says to himself as the figures are moved are a combination of what the storyteller said in the presentation and his own. Finally, he puts the material back on the shelf and steps back, looking at the material with a big smile on his face."

During the wondering period following the presentation of the day's lesson Bobby sat in silence, but he looked at children when they spoke and he listened intently to what they said.

During the time for responses Bobby made a painting of a figure in the center of the sheet of paper. It was two-thirds of the paper in height. The four additional figures were about one-third the height of the central figure and grouped around it. They were white. The large, central figure was brown and in green. All the figures were painted inside a brown, closed shape that was made with fairly straight lines.

This is very brief, but you can see how this is a description of what we can see from the outside. An effort is made not to make any conclusions about what is going on. Only what can be known by the senses is listed. No mental inferences were made.

I have saved the slides of children's art work for over twenty-five years. The art cannot be adequately described in words. Words are useful primarily to record what the children say about their art response.

To discover more about the child's mind-knowing we need to pay attention to the verbal wondering that is done in the group. We need to see what Bobby said about his painting of the figures inside the space enclosed by the brown lines. We need to ask ourselves, "What was Bobby thinking about?"

The mental aspect of what Bobby is doing is further clarified when it is compared to what other children have said. A developmental scheme can be constructed for the way children encounter existential issues with their minds. The scheme can then be compared to and tested by what other children say about the same thing.

It is also interesting to compare this kind of cognitive development with studies about how a child interacts with the natural world. The work of Jean Piaget, the great Swiss developmental psychologist, and his students comes immediately to mind.

A rough outline of the primary interests children have had when they worked with the Parable of the Good Shepherd has taken shape over the years.

- The youngest children, from about two to five or seven years old, tend to paint the Good Shepherd with the sheep inside the sheepfold.

- Children in middle childhood, around five or seven to nine years old, like to make the Good Shepherd a larger figure and show the sheep following him. The sheepfold drops out of their pictures and the connection between the large figure and the sheep becomes more interesting.
- The children in late childhood, about nine to twelve years old, are fascinated by the relationship between the Good Shepherd and the Ordinary (or mercenary) Shepherd. They like to think about what is different about these two figures and the way each relates to the sheep.

This is all very interesting, but it does not yet provide us with a way of knowing what has happened with regard to the presence of the mystery of God in the room. Thinking about things by making distinctions is not the same as being "with" or "in" them. Thinking about things keeps one at a distance.

To contemplate one needs to participate in what one is contemplating. Notice that Bonaventura called his treatise *The Soul's Journey into God.* It is not about the mind's thinking about God. It is about a journey, a process, by which one comes closer and closer to God and finally by grace one can be in God and God in us, or as St. Paul said "in Christ."

By this time you must be thinking that all of this is too much to expect from Sunday school. Isn't Sunday school to transfer the knowledge of the teacher to the minds of the children? Isn't that easier to do and to evaluate? The answer is, "Yes," but is that what we want?

Mind-knowing is what our century has emphasized. Body-knowing and spirit-knowing have not yet received their due, but the time is coming when we will have to pay attention to these kinds of knowing or we will cease to be human beings. We will become cybernetic hybrids of technology and biology without souls. We will lose the ability to love God with all our heart, mind, and soul, and to love our neighbors as ourselves.

Still, am I expecting too much? I want to respond with another question. Who said Sunday school was supposed to be trivial? Why does "the most wasted hour in the week" have to be wasted? Furthermore, just because religious education is serious does not mean it cannot make children happy. When a deep need is satisfied, human beings are happy. Learning the art of how to use religious language to make meaning satisfies a deep need. It is a need for both the children and the adult teachers.

The contemplation of the time spent with the children in religious education is very important. It is important for both the children and the teachers. Let us turn now to a description of how this might be done.

When you have straightened up the room, sit where you usually do as a storyteller or door person. Let the morning replay itself as you "suspend with wonder" the mind's ability to analyze what went on. Let the experience be. Enjoy it as a whole.

As you practice this the community of children will become more a part of your contemplation. One day you will become aware of the presence of the mystery of God in

95

that community as you are more fully present in the activity of the classroom. The awareness of the activity in the classroom stimulates your contemplation and your contemplation stimulates the awareness of what is happening in the classroom that is religious.

There will be some occasions when you will feel that it is not enough to merely sit and enjoy the recollection of what happened during the morning. Perhaps you will feel that there is more. The way into that larger or deeper sense of what happened for you is the same as for the children. Make an art response to the morning with the children. It needs to be done with the medium you are most comfortable using.

You already know at some level what you are going to make. As I say to the children, "Your fingers already know." Get out some paper, the clay, or other medium you feel fluent in and begin. Don't plan. Let the awareness come. Don't analyze what you are doing. That work of the mind will come later.

You might also sit in your place and become ready. Experiment with what this means. It is a kind of openness that is alert and ready. It is expectation. In Christian terms it is faith, hope, and love working in combination. When you are ready, get up and move around the room slowly until one of the materials calls to you. We often ask the children to do this. Now it is your turn.

Go toward the material that you are drawn to. This may have a special meaning for you that day. It may be the key to opening some door in your life that you have had to keep closed or someone else has locked. Present the material to yourself. Begin to wonder with yourself as you would with the children.

When your contemplation feels finished, sit back and enjoy it. After enjoying the wholeness of the contemplation it is time to allow your mind to begin its distinction-making. It is time to begin to analyze what you have done. This enables you to put into words something you can clarify to yourself and communicate to others. The mind gives you a way to discuss the morning with your colleague. What have you discovered about yourself and the children?

In addition, you can discuss how your contemplation of what happened compares with his or hers. It is great fun to see what each person has discovered through this process. It takes time, but this is a way to become better teachers, to be more aware of where your own journey is taking you, and, perhaps, even to enter the Kingdom that Jesus spoke of by knowing better what children know.

Let me be a little more precise about what this contemplative part of learning about what happened in the classroom is for. The goal is to make one's being and doing more in tune with each other. Your awareness of your action and the spirit of it can only become more aligned if you are aware of both. This awareness is not able to be tracked if you try to break it down into parts by evaluation. There are too many little parts. We need to call on our global intuition of what is happening and who we are to see how these two aspects of reality correspond. Reflecting on your being during moments of tranquillity allows this larger sense of who you are to surface. Your doing gradually will follow such an awareness, because it gives deep pleasure.

Reflection on the time spent with the children gives deep pleasure, because you become more integrated—body, mind, and spirit—as a living person. Seeking integration by either thinking or sensing or both lacks something. That "something" is spirit-knowing. For human development to become complete, this aspect of human knowing needs to be included, and working with children in this way is a good means to stimulate it.

Of course, we cannot be involved in everything that is needed for the children and for us to develop spiritually during one forty-five minute class each week. We need to connect with nature, our own deep self, others, and God's presence. This whole system of relationships gives us a home of meaning in which to live despite our absolute, existential limits as living creatures.

We need to go beyond thinking of health as the optimum functioning of the human being in our biological, psychological, or social dimensions. We need to add the spiritual dimension to our definition of health, because it entails a kind of life that can be healthy despite disease, abnormalities, economic reverses, and other events of the body or mind that can cause suffering and death.

The spiritual dimension adds to the definition of human health, because it involves us in a different kind of knowing from the knowing of the body by the senses, or the knowing of the mind by reason. The development of the knowing of the spirit by contemplation defines the area in which religious education can contribute to human health. This is what makes religious education unique and important.

We come now to the other kind of learning that is useful to see what has happened in the classroom during the morning. This is evaluation.

# Evaluating the Children's "Work"

When you and your colleague have finished your reflection in tranquillity it is time to evaluate the morning. This is a different kind of learning from the contemplative method. You no longer suspend the mind with wonder. You begin to use the mind not only to remember details but to make an analysis of what went on.

Remember that the children's "work," is serious play, deep play. It is work because the work being done is the construction of the child's spiritual knowing. The spiritual knowing is stimulated by the co-teachers' attitudes, the language of the Christian people, and the presence of the mystery of God.

The goal of this evaluation is to determine how well the children have been drawn into the cretive process to make the language of the Christian people their own. This is important because this special language invites us to approach God in an indirect way so we will not be overwhelmed.

For religious language to do its job as a tool for the making of meaning about our existential situation, we need to "enter" it deeply. This means that our evaluation must include a measure of how much of the creative process is being used by the child and how deeply the child is involved with the language that is presented.

# The Creative Process in Worship and Education

The process goes something like this: One begins with an assumed closure, a kind of circle of meaning that one lives with as part of his or her reality. We have many such "closures." They are related to aspects of existence ranging from what one is going to have for supper this evening to what one is going to do with his or her life.

When the circle of assumed meaning is broken by some kind of crisis or "dissolved" by wonder, the conclusion is no longer tenable. What was an assumed meaning now becomes a problem. The now open question throbs in one's awareness or at other levels that are not conscious. This discomfort prompts one to scan the horizon of possible meanings to see if there is some way to put the old circle of coherence back together again.

Once an assumed meaning is broken it becomes a problem and can't be put back together again in the same old way. This is the fact of Humpty Dumpty. A broken problem won't "go away" or become part of one's assumed world until it is solved (or coped with if it turns out to be an existential issue).

A new form needs to be discovered that incorporates both the "reality" of the old closure and the features of the new situation that broke up the old meaning. This discovery process is what drives human development as well as motivates the heroes of the imagination, some of the greatest of whom Daniel J. Boorstin described in his book *The Creators*.

This discovery process or scanning can last for a few moments, weeks, months, years—who knows? It continues until there is an insight. One of the curious things about the insight is that it often becomes known to be "there" by a shift of energy before one knows what it is.

How does the insight get drawn into consciousness? The energy invested in the scanning shifts to the articulation of the insight. The form of the insight might begin as a bit of a song, a piece of a picture, a fragment of a dream, or some other part of the whole new circle of meaning. It sometimes takes a great deal of work and time to develop the whole idea from the fragment one first becomes aware of.

The development of the idea brings the insight from its more symbolic stage to a more literal and limited kind of statement. At first the person who had the insight might be the only one able to take any meaning from it, but later it becomes an idea that can be communicated and known by others. This more complete articulation of the insight gives others the opportunity to help you test and better articulate the idea.

The process of articulation can go on forever. For example, some people have a difficult time letting go of their creations. A manuscript is never perfect enough to be published, or a painting is never finished enough to be shown. Finally, one has to make an act of will and say that the insight is articulated in finished-enough form. When it is time to conclude depends on the method of verification used and the personality of the person articulating the idea.

The creative process is a theme that runs all through our biological, psychological, social, and spiritual lives, but in the Holy Eucharist it is especially available for our spiritual lives.

We come in and prepare to be challenged by the Word of God. We open our minds. We begin to wonder. The lessons and the sermon come at us from a perspective that is not that of our everyday lives. It often breaks our ordinary circle of meaning in a crisis or dissolves it by wonder. The music, the symbols, and the whole setting work together to help in this process.

The breaking up or dissolving of our assumed, conscious meaning can be overwhelming. We need others around us to help us endure this by their presence and wisdom. We need a safe place for ultimate meaning to be made.

In the church we have a community of pilgrims and the structure of the liturgy to help us. The liturgy gives us a form in which to let ourselves go to find new meaning. It is a place where we can become more deeply aware of God's presence during the in-between times when meaning seems impossible. Such a safe place is important if we are going to risk coming apart ourselves to know what God would have us do in the future and who we truly are.

The worship of many Christian people includes a moment, usually after the sermon, when we say together what we believe. Since there are so many interpretations of the Creed, it might be better to say that we say together that we are united despite these many interpretations. We affirm that we can be together no matter how broken we might be. This community of faith, hope, and love can help see us through.

Holy Communion comes after the challenge of and reflection on God's Word, because one may not be able to complete the cycle of the creative process in a short period of education or the time of worship with the community. The shape of the classical liturgy shows that even if there are questions asked that have no answers in ordinary terms they do have an answer in the experience of God's presence in Holy Communion.

Christian worship gives us a time, a language, and a place to look at who we are called to be. When we conclude Holy Communion and everything is put away in the church (as in the classroom where we can learn this art), it is time to say good-bye. We receive a blessing and are sent on our way to continue our journey, to work out our salvation with diligence and grace.

It is important for the child to be able to follow through the whole process of creativity to be able to communicate with God and others in a worshiping community. The structure of worship draws on the whole process to help us meet the Creator.

People sometimes have resistance to different aspects of the creative process. The teacher needs to be aware of this in order to help the children move through these blockages.

## The Creative Process and Personality Preferences

We need to find a way to help children with different personality types step more fully into the life process of the Christian people. We need to be able to support the whole dynamic of life that the Creator has given us, because we are created in the image of the One who creates. It is our true identity.

If we return to the opening of the creative process and follow it to completion while commenting on personality types, we find that some people actually enjoy the scanning process. They like to journey out into uncharted areas. Others find this process unthinkable. Naturally, it is hard to get a child or adult who likes to be in control of where they are and wants to stay in control to scan. While in the scanning process, you lose control and do not know where you will end up. You are in the wilderness.

The danger of the wilderness is that you may not find your way out. You might wander for more than forty years. There are people that are perpetually lost. Something in their personality does not equip them to be at home in a new place. There are those who will never ask the great questions of themselves, because the risk of exploring seems too overwhelming.

People sometimes can withstand the scanning process because they like the excitement of the journey. They like to or are compelled to move forward into the unknown. Others are willing to endure the wilderness because of the insight that brings the scanning process to completion.

For some, discovery is thrilling and worth the journey, but for others such an event is too unsettling. They prefer the old way. They want to go back. A new insight is not enough of a reward to merit living through the anxiety of the scanning. What would you do with a new insight anyway?

Among the people who enjoy making discoveries are those who don't care whether they communicate their insight to anyone else or not. They also do not care if what they have found is tested and validated by other sources or processes. Their interest is in the excitement of the discovery itself. That is what motivates them. Besides, they know what they know.

Others who also enjoy the experience of insight enjoy communicating their discovery to others. They are as interested in the communication as they are in the discovery itself. Some want to know what others think. Others want people to agree with them.

In addition to the types of people already mentioned, there are some who do not like scanning or insight-making. They like to have someone else bring them a new idea. Their enjoyment comes from figuring out the best way to communicate these ideas. There is a natural division of labor between idea people and those who like to work out ways to communicate ideas. It takes so much energy to come up with the new ideas that sometimes little energy is left to communicate and validate them. This division of labor is very useful and practical.

Finally, there are people who do not like scanning, insight-making, or the communication of new ideas. They like to sit back and make decisions about what is a good idea and what is a good way to communicate it. They are much like computers. They only like to say "Yes" or "No." They like to have their will tested and see that things get done when they say, "Yes."

Children as well as adults display preferences for different parts of this creative process. The first step in evaluation, then, is to ask yourself which children are which type. This determination will help us help the children carry their work all the way through the process to completion. The completion of this cycle can be so satisfying that it will become self-reinforcing in time.

- Children who only *like to sit back and say "Yes" or "No"* (usually "No" or "Boring") need to have their circle of meaning broken by crisis or dissolved by wonder. We have a responsibility to help such children continue though the whole process to discover new things about themselves and life and communicate them. We don't shake up such children just to see them uncomfortable. We do this to help them get the process started. We then need to be sure that we help them carry it through to completion.

101

- The children categorized as *scanners* need to be helped to make insights. Is the wandering around the classroom constructive or destructive? We need to help them find the excitement of making discoveries.
- The *insight-makers* need a lot of support to communicate their discoveries to others and to test them. They need different ways to express their ideas and evaluate them. This helps them move forward in the process toward completion of the cycle.
- The *binary decision-makers* need to be moved into scanning and brought clear around the circle of the process back to what they like best. They will never understand the people who discover new ideas unless they too spend some time in the wilderness. More important, they will stay stuck, even if their way of life is constructive in the beginning. Being stuck for too long becomes destructive. It is the whole process that gives us life, not just the exercise of the will at the end. Life is more than willpower.

In addition to keeping track of children's preferences for this or that part of the creative process, we also need to be aware of each child's depth of creative concentration. This can help us see how best to support the child's ability to enter the parables, sacred stories, and liturgical action of the Christian tradition.

# The Depth of Creative Concentration

The depth of a child's creative concentration needs to be a continuing concern of both the storyteller and the doorperson. Sometimes activity that looks and sounds like chaos may be a defense mechanism. A child may not want to enter the story. It is too risky. Other times a disturbance might be an attempt to take over the leadership of the classroom. Loud or agitated intrusions also might be the result of an insight. It can indicate exuberance, not misbehavior. How does one tell the difference?

The time and energy devoted to getting ready in the classroom is an invitation to the children to enter into deep concentration. The materials, the environment, and the management of a Godly Play classroom are designed especially to help with this. The use of rugs, the underlays for the materials, the use of the circle, the uncluttering of the room, and much more all help promote concentration.

Deep concentration is important for the religious language we have inherited to do its work. Children or adults who skate easily across the surface of the worship experience have little appreciation for what depths upon depths of meaning are available there for them.

Concentration takes courage and we adults need to acknowledge this. Making a safe place and being a safe and trustworthy person are critical to working with children's misbehavior that is grounded in the defensiveness of lost courage.

102

To deeply concentrate means that you do not attend to potential dangers around you. You do not attend to movement from children or teachers, not even to the flicker in the light or birds flying by the window.

Scattered concentration might be called *level one*. Focused but easily distracted attention might be called *level two*. *Level three* is deep concentration. Noticing these levels helps the teacher move children in the right direction toward deeper concentration. It is also a way to take note of your own level of concentration and that of the community of children. It is a diagnostic tool for discovering what may be blocking the spiritual development of you and the children.

The goal of this focused energy also needs to be constructive. One can be focused on disrupting the circle. That takes concentration, but it does not contribute to the creativity of the whole group. It is focused energy but destructive.

One particular kind of destructive concentration deserves special mention, because it often is overlooked. Some children withdraw into themselves. They will not take the chance of entering into the lesson or the group. Soon they shut down relationships and try to shut down their own emotions. These children do not cause problems, but their deep concentration is destructive. It maintains a pause in the process of life. The child's energy will wind down. Exuberance, discovery, and an openness about themselves and the presence of God is closed off. Disintegration rather than integration will be the result. This is why teaching children only to be nice and quiet in Sunday school can be dangerous.

The Godly Play approach to classroom management teaches for long-term growth. The important years of childhood are the focus, because an attitude toward religion and the child's involvement in God's Creation is being established at this time, whether we adults are intentional about it or not.

In the evaluation process we have now looked at the need to keep in mind the various kinds of preferences children and adults have for the steps in the creative process. This is so we can help children integrate the whole process into their lives. In addition, we looked at the need for keeping track of the children's depth of concentration. This is to help us see where problems may arise in the community of children's ability to enter into the language of the Christian people. We turn now to a scheme for record-keeping that integrates these concerns with what the children are actually working on in the classroom.

# Cautious Record Keeping

It is not hard to remember the things that the children do on a Sunday morning, but when you look back over several Sundays or several years of Sundays it becomes more difficult. To think clearly about an individual child or a group of children you need a way to aid your memory and intuitions as well as to keep your memory from playing tricks on you.

Keeping track of what the children are doing and have done is research, but you don't have to do this to prove anything. The kind of record-keeping I describe will not snap heads around if you are talking to educational research people. It is very "soft" and subjective. *The best reason I can think of to keep records is that it helps you sharpen your sensitivity to the children and to yourself. It helps you improve as a teacher.*

There are some other good reasons for keeping track of what the children have done in the classroom. **Such records are very helpful to rely on for parent conferences, which sometimes can be emotional encounters.**

Some parents will come to see you merely to find out how their children are doing. They are interested, trust you, understand the curriculum, and merely want to be brought up to date. You usually don't see many of these parents. You also don't see many of the parents who are not well informed but are reasonably happy. Unfortunately, the parents you are most likely to see are the ones who come to air their complaints and express their anxiety about what is going on. These are the times that it is especially nice to have good records to rely on.

A good set of recorded facts about a child can move an emotional discussion toward one of perspective and reason. Rather than swimming in feelings and projected feelings you can point to the record. You can ask the parent to be specific and not to be so general in his or her assertions. Examples of the behavior you have noticed can be substantiated over several Sundays and sometimes over several years.

One of the most important things to remember about your record-keeping is that the parents have not given you permission to use their children as research subjects or to comment on their behavior without their agreement.

For my research classes the parents sign consent forms. These classes are two hours long and meet on Saturday for that stated purpose. Parents give me permission in writing to do research and to report on what their children do and say.

Another thing to remember about your record-keeping is that teachers *describe* what children do. Mental health professionals and physicians diagnose and treat mental health problems.

You diagnose and treat *educational* problems. Sometimes a family mental health problem can disrupt a child's learning. The areas of concern are close and in many cases overlap, so the rule of thumb about only describing events is important to keep in mind.

You may be asked by the parents to work with a mental health professional or a physician to describe behavior you have experienced in the classroom. Your notes can help you do this with accuracy and competence.

Being able to describe a child's behavior is very important, since many people engaged in mental health do not have an opportunity to see a total picture of a child's life. They depend on their skill at making judgments with a high probability about what goes on outside of their office observations and testing. Your view of the child may be needed to fill in information gaps and to test hypotheses.

Sometimes you may see things you really don't want to see. For example, you may see suggestions of child abuse. A child might dodge when you raise your hand to scratch your head or you may find suspicious wounds on a child. These matters should be discussed with your co-teacher first to see if he or she has noticed the same things. You also need to describe what you have seen to the senior clergyperson at your church. There may be a law in your state mandating the report of any suspected child abuse. Contact your local law enforcement or children's services agency for information.

The fewer people who become involved with this kind of information the better, but you don't want to leave out the person in charge of the Sunday school if there is one. It is a good idea for you and your coteacher to go see the senior minister with that person.

There are two good reasons to make your official report in the company of colleagues. One is to be sure that you have someone to corroborate your observation. The second reason is to have someone with you to substantiate that you did report this and what happened in that interview.

You should report your observations to the senior minister because he or she may already be working with the child's family. It will be a great help to the pastor to have this information to enlarge his or her information. Again, your ability to be clear and factual about your description is very helpful. Of course, all parties will keep this information in the strictest confidence.

You will notice that I assume a high degree of competence on the part of the clergy. This is a delicate situation. The way in which a clergyperson responds to such matters varies according to the church tradition and the person's professional training. I also assume an ability and a willingness of the minister to work with mental health people and physicians. The way this cooperation is carried out also varies, but the clergyperson is very important to the success of getting the right kind of help for the family.

Early warning signs of families in crisis is another reality in the Sunday school that many overlook. In Godly Play classrooms we don't just talk about how Christian people ought to live, we show this every Sunday and find ways to care responsibly even when that is hard. This includes our effort to help the child's family within our limitations as teachers.

With all of this in mind we now can turn to a description of how to make a record about your time with the children. You can't write down everything a child says and does, so you need a system.

# Recording Long-term Spiritual Growth

Your system of record-keeping cannot be so complicated that you are overwhelmed and never keep records. It must be right for you and doable. What follows are some sug-

**Helpful Hint:**

Place a clipboard with one sheet of paper for each child in a convenient place in the room. It should be placed high enough to be kept out of the reach of the children. Make your notes here when it does not intrude on the class. Sometimes you will have to wait until right after the class when the children are gone.

On each sheet of paper write the name of one child. Down the left side of the paper list the names of each material in the room that is available for the children to work with. Across the top of the paper write: *Lesson, Presented, Exploring,* and *Integrated.* You also need room at the bottom to make additional notes that do not fit into the categories listed above.

gestions for how to do this in the unique setting of religious education.

Under the *Presented* column note the date a child is presented a lesson. One way for a presentation to occur is during the lesson for the day. Another way for this to happen is if a child is unable to make up his or her mind about what work to get out and receives a special lesson after the main one. There also are lessons that children who have had a lesson give to a child who has not yet had it.

When children have an opportunity to choose their own work, you enter what they select to work on in the column marked *Exploring* and date it. Exploring includes getting a material off a shelf and presenting it to oneself or working with a small group. It may be making an art response to a particular material, or watching another child or group of children working with something. Comments of children during the wondering can be entered and dated at the bottom of the page where there is room, and linked to the presentation wondered about.

The *Exploring* column may have several notes and dates in it. Sometimes children go back to a material because it is familiar. Their concentration may not be deep for that. They use these familiar materials to sort of "warm up" for their "big work," reading deep concentration, that will come later. What we are interested in here is observing as the child scans, gains insight, learns how to articulate the insight, and then adds this bit of wisdom to his or her worldview.

The final column, *Integrated,* is where you note the material and

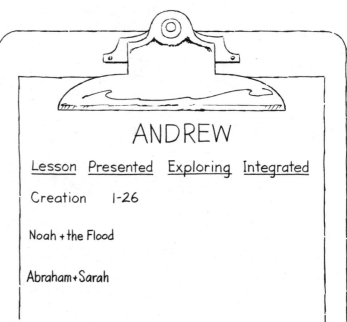

the date when a child applies a material to a situation in his or her life. It is also where you mark when a child spontaneously presents a particular material to another child, which suggests the child has become fluent in its use. It is likely that this kind of use will continue to deepen and broaden throughout the child's life if the creative process has been engaged.

This record-keeping system will make the most sense in a Godly Play, open access classroom where parable, sacred story and liturgy are made into hands-on materials, for the lessons and for the children to use during their work. Since these materials actually sit on the shelves around the room, you can literally see what children are working on by what they take off the shelves. This form of record-keeping may also be adapted to whatever curriculum you are using.

The record sheets will accumulate for each child as he or she moves through your church school. This way you will be able to see which child has had which lessons. Since children do not come every Sunday, there are often gaps in their learning. You can fill these gaps if you know what they are.

The language of the Christian people can stimulate us over and over again as we change and encounter new situations. We begin to scan again, search for new insight, articulate that insight to others and to add new meaning to our storehouse of useful knowledge for the journey of life.

This kind of evaluation is interesting, because it sharpens the awareness of teachers about both the children and themselves. It also helps teachers see what materials are appropriate and useful for the children. When one is teaching for long-term growth these records are passed on from teacher to teacher.

In programs where several curricula are used for early, middle, and late childhood the record-keeping needs to be refined to show what you would like the children to learn overall during their church school years. This list can be written down the left-hand side of each sheet under *Materials,* although you might prefer to call these *Goals.*

Much teacher burnout in religious education comes from two major misunderstandings. The first misunderstand, develops because teachers often feel that their work is not respected or even appreciated. In response, many churches and schools go out of their way to shower teachers with parties and presents. Despite parties and presents, teachers continue to burn out.

The second concern is that teachers in the church school are taken away from adult education opportunities and even church! Working with children begins to be considered a block or at least a hindrance to an adult's spiritual growth. To counteract this perception teachers are asked to teach for only short periods of time. Although everyone knows that this is not good for the children, this is the compromise that is reached between the needs of the children and the adults.

Using the Godly Play method to teach renews the spirituality of the adult teachers, which in turn stimulates the spiritual growth of the children, which in turn again stimulates the adult's spiritual growth. The teachers learn from the children by reflection and evaluation, and continue growing so they do not burn out. Their spirits are being nourished in a very appropriate way, so they don't need other kinds of recognition or rewards.

The Godly Play method illustrates how important the teachers' work is, no matter what notice is taken of it, because it is critical for the growth of both the children and the adults.

In terms of spiritual growth, the teachers in the church school working with the children are the lucky ones, not those in adult education. The children are the ones most likely to stun you into understanding Jesus' parable of action. Setting a child in the midst of adults can have remarkable results. Setting an adult in the midst of children may be even more profound.

# Appendix

# Responsibilities of the Doorperson

❑ Check the shelves, especially the supply shelves and art shelves.

❑ Get out roll book, review notes, and get ready to greet the children and parents.

❑ Slow down the children coming into the room. Help them get ready to take the roll or have the older children check themselves in.

❑ Close the door when it is time, and be ready to work with latecomers and children who come to you from the circle.

❑ Avoid casual eye contact with the storyteller to help prevent the adults in the room from turning the children into objects, talking down to them or manipulating them.

❑ When the children choose their work listen so you can help them help themselves get out their work. They need help setting up their art work and getting from the shelves what they need to work on a lesson either alone or in a small group.

❑ Stay in your chair unless children need your help. Do not intrude on the community of children. Stay down at the eye level of the children when it is possible.

❑ Help the children help themselves put their work away and also help the children get ready who are going to serve the feast.

❑ Sit quietly in your chair during the feast and be sure that the trash can has a plastic liner in it.

❑ Greet the parents and begin to call the names of the children whose parents are there and who are ready to leave.

❑ If a child starts for the door without saying good-bye to the storyteller, remind him or her to say good-bye to the storyteller.

❑ Remember to give back things that may have been taken at the beginning of class.

❑ When all the children have gone, check the art and supply shelves and clean up.

❑ Sit and quietly comtemplate the class as a whole.

❑ Evaluate, make notes, and discuss the class with your co-teacher.

# Responsibilities of the Storyteller

❏ Check the material to be presented that day.

❏ Get seated on the floor in the circle and prepare to greet the children.

❏ Guide the children to places in the circle where they will best be able to attend to the lesson. Visit quietly until it is time to begin and all are ready.

❏ Present the lesson. Model how to "enter" the material.

❏ Draw the children into the lesson by your introduction and bringing your gaze down to focus on the material when you begin the actual lesson.

❏ After the lesson, go around the circle and dismiss each child one at a time to get his or her work. Go quickly around the circle on the first round then return to children who cannot decide. Go around the circle for decisions until only a few are left, who may be new or for some other reason cannot make choices. Present them a lesson.

❏ Remain seated in the circle unless children need help with lessons they have gotten out. You also may need to help with the art materials. Keep down at the child's eye level.

❏ When it is time for the feast, go to the light switch and turn it off. Ask the children to put their work away and come to the circle for the feast. Turn the light back on. Then go to the circle to anchor it as children finish and return there for the feast.

❏ Ask for but do not pressure the prayers. After the feast show the children how to put their things in the trash.

❏ Help the children get ready to have their names called.

❏ When the children have their names called they come to you. You hold out your hands. They take them if they wish, and you tell them privately that they did good work, are wonderful, and to come back when they can.

❑ Take time to enjoy saying good-bye.

❑ When all are gone, check the material shelves and clean the room.

❑ Sit and quietly contemplate the class as a whole.

❑ Evaluate, make notes, and discuss with your co-teacher.

 # Supplies

## Cleaning Supplies

- ☐ One roll of paper towels
- ☐ One feather duster
- ☐ One set: brush and dustpan
- ☐ One spray bottle on tray with sponge and clean cloth
- ☐ One basket for dirty cloths
- ☐ One basket for clean cloths
- ☐ One bucket with small pitcher, sponge, drying cloth, and 12″ X 18″ plastic underlay rolled up inside
- ☐ One trashcan with plastic liner

## Feast Supplies

- ☐ Napkins (perhaps the color of the liturgical season)
- ☐ Basket for serving food such as cookies, various breads, etc.
- ☐ Cookies or various breads for the liturgical season
- ☐ Tray for serving in small cups
- ☐ Small cups
- ☐ Pitcher for pouring into the small cups from juice cans or other large containers

## Art Supplies

- [ ] Four white painting trays with sides about 30″ X 30″
- [ ] Four drawing boards about 30″ X 30″
- [ ] Three clay boards about six inches in diameter
- [ ] Three clay containers about two cups in size with sealed tops
- [ ] Basketful of clay tools, both wood and metal
- [ ] Good quality nontoxic clay that can be baked at home in the oven and dries white
- [ ] Mat boards for special paintings by the children
- [ ] Four trays with places for five or six round containers of tempera paint that can be sealed and have one hole in top (so only a single paintbrush can be used for a color at a time)
- [ ] Wood plaques for mounting clay objects which will not stand up on their own (so they can be hung up on the wall)
- [ ] One basket of wood scraps
- [ ] One basket of a variety of cloth scraps
- [ ] One basket of various kinds of wire
- [ ] Various colors of nontoxic acrylic paints
- [ ] Two containers for mixed colors of thin markers
- [ ] Two containers for mixed colors of fat markers
- [ ] Two containers for mixed colors of pencils
- [ ] One container of regular pencils
- [ ] One sharpener for the pencils (electric is best when it is possible)
- [ ] One box with small file drawers with erasers, paper clips, staples, etc.
- [ ] One small basket with scissors
- [ ] Three rulers in a long basket or tray
- [ ] One basket with glue and glue sticks
- [ ] One basket with two clear tape dispensers
- [ ] One basket with clear plastic underlays rolled up in it to be used for clay and other work that might harm the working surfaces
- [ ] One basket or tray with polish, underlay, and polishing cloth for metal
- [ ] Several books with blank pages to be used for journals by older children
- [ ] Several sheets of "big paper" about 12″ X 18″
- [ ] Several sheets of "small paper" about 9″ X 12″
- [ ] Four trays for watercolors, each with a paint tray, brush, sponge, and water container with a lid

# Furniture

1. One special altar shelf that is a bit lower and wider than the regular shelves (No shelf should be over 36″ high.)

   A. Regular Shelves for an Established Classroom (No shelf should be over 36″ high.)
      - one Christmas shelf
      - one Easter shelf
      - three Old Testament shelves
      - three New Testament shelves
      - one saints shelf
      - one special shelf for desert box to fit under, etc.
      - one special shelf for the parable of the church
      - two parable shelves
      - two supply shelves
      - one set of liturgical furniture
      - one shelf for Bibles and the story of the Bible
      - two sets of shelves or closet for work in progress (for safe keeping)

   OR

   B. Regular Shelves for a Beginning Classroom (No shelf should be over 36″ high.)
      - one focal shelf
      - one sacred story shelf
      - one parable shelf
      - one liturgy shelf (many liturgical items are on the focal shelf)
      - two art supply shelves
      - one supply shelf
      - one shelf or closet for work in progress (for safe keeping)

2. Rug Box

This contains six rugs that are bound and about 3′ x 4′ in size.
(Please use solid colors with a good depth to them. These need to
be substantial, feel good, and look beautiful to give the place for working its
proper value. Roll them so the colored side is outside.)

# Lesson Materials

1. Prayerfully find the heart or core of the story, parable, or liturgical event.

2. Develop a full bibliography and read widely about the observations of biblical scholars and theologians from the early church to the present. The history of interpretation is important to understand for perspective.

3. Decide what your biblical theology is and the criteria by which you select one story, parable, or liturgical event over another.

4. Decide what medium is best to render the image in.

5. Fashion the image.

6. Present the material to experienced adult teachers for their comments.

7. Test with children for about five years, using this seven step process:
   - If children do not spontaneously use the material become suspicious.
   - Check your own attitude toward the material and presentation.
   - Check the words of the presentation. Use words children use when speaking to each other without awareness of adult listening.
   - Check the material itself. Is it open to all the stages of faith development?
   - Check the movements of the presentation.
   - Read again widely about the story, liturgical act, or parable.
   - If children still do not spontaneously use the material discard it.

8. You also might call 1-800-445-4390 to see if Godly Play Resources makes the kind of material you are looking for. Our materials have already met the above tests. The address is: P.O. Box 563, Ashland, KS 67831 if you care to write.